RÂMA AND HOMER

RÂMA AND HOMER:

AN ARGUMENT THAT IN THE INDIAN EPICS HOMER FOUND THE THEME OF HIS TWO GREAT POEMS

ARTHUR LILLIE

GYAN

Published by

Gyan Publishing House
5, Ansari Road
Daryaganj, New Delhi-110002
Phone: 011-47034999, 9811692060
E-mail: books@gyanbooks.com

Distribution Network
gyanbooks.com
India, USA, Canada, UK, Australia

ISBN: 978-93-6920-390-1 (PB)
First Published, 1912

2nd Impression 2025

Printed at: Gyan Press, Delhi.

RÂMA AND HOMER
Author: ARTHUR LILLIE

RÂMA AND HOMER

RÂMA AND SÎTÂ (OLD ROCK TEMPLE ELVRA) [Frontispiece

(From a drawing by William Daniell, R.A.)

RÂMA AND HOMER

AN ARGUMENT THAT IN THE INDIAN EPICS HOMER FOUND THE THEME OF HIS TWO GREAT POEMS

BY

ARTHUR LILLIE

(Late Regiment of Lucknow)

AUTHOR OF

"BUDDHISM IN CHRISTENDOM," "BUDDHA AND BUDDHISM," "INDIA IN PRIMITIVE CHRISTIANITY," ETC.

LONDON

KEGAN PAUL, TRENCH, TRÜBNER & CO., LTD.

BROADWAY HOUSE, 68-74, CARTER LANE, E.C.

1912

PREFACE

SEEING a posthumous book through the press is a task not to be lightly undertaken, and more especially does this apply to a work like "Râma and Homer," requiring an expert's knowledge, to which I certainly make no pretension. For the author it is a comparatively easy matter to lay his finger upon a particular book, a particular passage, so well does he know his way about, and until the finishing touches are given the merest notes are all-sufficing in the way of references. It is these "finishing" touches which an alien hand finds so perplexing.

When I was told that my old friend, the late Mr. Arthur Lillie, had in his last brief illness expressed a wish—a wish conveyed to me after his death in November, 1911—that I should undertake this task, knowing, as I well did from our many talks, how near to his heart the subject lay, it will be readily understood that, in spite of these perplexities and difficulties, any idea of shirking the responsibility was, of course, out of the question.

We can but deeply regret that he who brought to his work the deep study and extensive knowledge contained in "Râma and Homer" did not survive to see in print this last product of his life's labour.

One indulgence I hope I may beg from the reader—that whatever shortcomings are discovered in this volume, the blame shall rest upon myself and not upon the author, whose previous works gained him so high a reputation.

To Miss Hughes, Secretary of the Royal Asiatic Society, and to Dr. Kapádia, Lecturer to the University of London, I am greatly indebted, and desire here to express my sincere thanks to both for much kind assistance in the Oriental spelling and accentuation.

G. KEITH MURRAY.

March, 1912.

CONTENTS

CHAPTER I

STORY OF MENELAUS

CHAPTER II

STORY OF ACHILLES

CHAPTER IV

STORY OF THE "RÂMÂYAṆA"

CHAPTER V

STORY OF RÂMA (*continued*): IN THE FOREST

CHAPTER VI

RÂMA'S BRIDGE

CHAPTER VII

EVIDENCE OF DION CHRYSOSTOMOS

CHAPTER VIII

THE EVIDENCE OF THE "ZEND AVESTA"

CHAPTER IX

THE EVIDENCE FROM GREECE

CHAPTER X

ANIMAL WORSHIP

CHAPTER XI

A PREGNANT DISCOVERY

CHAPTER XII

COLONEL TOD

LIST OF ILLUSTRATIONS

RÂMA AND HOMER

CHAPTER I

STORY OF MENELAUS

THE "Iliad" gives an account of three battles, but there is a strange fact which Mr. Wilkins has lately pointed out very distinctly. Hour for hour two distinct campaigns are being carried on.[1] With one—which I will call the "Story of Menelaus"—the victory, Jove-aided, is with the Greeks. With the other—which I will call the "Story of Achilles"—the victory for the first two days is with the Trojans, and Jove is a strong partisan on their side:

> "None stand so dear to Jove as sacred Troy,
> No mortals merit more distinguished grace
> Than god-like Priam, or than Priam's race."

---

[1] Wilkins, "Growth of the Homeric Poems," p. 52.

Jove holds up golden scales which always decide against the Greeks.

To make all this more intelligible, I have drawn up what I call a "Coincidence Time-chart."

COINCIDENCE TIME-CHART.

STORY OF MENELAUS	STORY OF ACHILLES.
Fighting begins twenty-third day of tenth year.	Fighting begins twenty-third day of tenth year.
First Day's Battle.	*First Day's Battle.*
Single combat between Menelaus and Paris, arranged to end the war. Paris, vanquished, flies. Menelaus treacherously wounded. This angers Jupiter. The truce is broken, and the Trojans fly before the Greeks. "E'en god-like Hector seems himself to fear, Slow he gave way, the rest tumultuous fled." At night, says Pope, "Jupiter disheartens the Trojans with thunder and other signs of his wrath."	Single combat between Ajax and Hector, stopped by heralds. Hector has driven the Greeks to their ships. Menelaus, not knowing that he has been in any way wounded, puts on his armour to fight Hector. The other chiefs treat him as incompetent; and nine of them draw lots for the venture, Agamemnon, Diomedes, Ulysses, the Ajaces, etc. The Greeks raise up hasty entrenchments by the ships.
[*Five days' rest.*]	[*Five days' rest.*]

Second Day's Battle (twenty-ninth day of the year).

Agamemnon attacks the Trojans; and at noon forces their lines at the Tumulus of Ilus. He chases them to the beech-tree near the Scæan Gates. This, being five miles off, would require all the remaining daylight.

Second Day's Battle (twenty-ninth day of the year).

Hector forces the Greek entrenchments and burns some of the ships. Patroclus dresses up in the armour of Achilles and is killed.

The third day, the thirtieth day of the tenth year, Achilles kills Hector; but that, we know, did not end the war. Paris, the ravisher, could only be killed by the arrow of Philoctetes. In point of fact he killed Achilles.

These contradictions have been accounted for by a theory of two wings being engaged; but it is plain that one account has been purposely plastered over another.

In Homer are three stories; which I will call the "Story of Menelaus," the "Story of Achilles," and the "Story of Ulysses." I believe that all three have been derived from Vâlmîki's "Râmâyaṇa."

Let us compare the "Story of Menelaus" with this.

1. The heroes of the one are two Greek brothers who are never separated. The heroes of the other are two Hindu brothers who are never separated.

2. The Greeks have been banished from Argos, their kingdom, by their usurping uncle Thyestes. The Hindus have been banished from their kingdom of Ayodhyâ (Oude) by the intrigues of one of the favourite wives of their father.

3. Jousts are held in India for the espousals of a beautiful woman. She is the daughter of Sîtâ, or Brahmî, Brahmâ's wife; and is called Sîtâ after her mother. The Hindus gave to each god an emblematical animal on which his Śakti, or female energy, was supposed to ride. Brahmî rode upon a swan; and Sîtâ (lit., furrow) was the furrow that held the swan's egg. Sîtâ, according to the Indian myth, was found in a furrow. Much the same thing is said of Helen. Mr. Bryant shows that she also

came from a swan's egg left by her mother, Leda, the swan.[1]

4. At the "Svayam̃vara," as it is called, Râma defeats all the competing princes and wins the bride. In Greece, Menelaus defeats all competing princes and wins Helen. Mr. Mahaffy, a profound Homeric student, tells us that the jousts described by Homer differ completely from "the Olympic games, the oldest historical contests of the same kind known to us" ("Problems in Greek History," p. 46). Helen is allowed to choose her husband, which is not a Greek custom, although it is an Indian one. The word "Svayam̃vara" in Sanskrit means "the maiden's choice."

5. Whilst the husbands are absent Paris comes and steals away Helen, and Râvaṇa comes and steals away Sîtâ. Helen is carried away across the sea to Troy. Sîtâ is carried away across the sea to Laṅkâ (Ceylon). At this date the husbands have become paramount Kings.

[1] There was a controversy over the name of her birthplace, ὑπερωον (Bryant, "Dissertation on the Trojan War," pp. 10, 11).

6. "Ilion's lofty Towers" are on high ground dominating a plain. The city of Laṅkâ is on high ground dominating a plain.

7. A lengthy muster roll of the forces is given in the sixth book of "Râmâyaṇa," and Professor Monier Williams has drawn attention to the analogy between this and that of the Greek forces in the "Iliad."

8. Priam on a high tower above the Scæan Gate gets Helen to point out the chief Greek captains one by one. Vibhîshaṇa from a high hill points out to Râma the principal warriors of the "Wanderers of the Night" (the forces of Râvaṇa). Here we seem to get a derived incident. Surely in nine years Priam could have discovered the names of the Greek heroes without Helen's help.

9. The army of Râma, like all armies in Indian records, is enormous; and the Hindu warriors fight in chariots, probably the earliest expedient thought of by the Âryas to utilize their favourite animal, the horse. The Greek army is also enormous. Grote

fixes it at 100,000 men! The number of ships, 1,186, which were required for its carriage is questioned by Mr. Bryant, who points out that when a really historical danger threatened the Greek states, as at Artemiseum, they could only concentrate 271 ships and six or seven Pentecontores.[1]

10. Mr. Wilkins shows that Achilles fights on foot, and so do Ajax and Hector, and Hector and Patroclus.

In all their battles, though chariots are sometimes mentioned, yet we nowhere find any clear conception of their use in the fight.[2] This seems certainly confirmed in the "Odyssey." In the jousts there described there are no chariot-races at all.

11. M. Fauche points out that the title "Anax Anacton" applied to Agamemnon is used in the Indian version to describe Sugrîva, the Indian chief.

12. The arrows of Hector and the arrows of Râvaṇa[3] come back to the hand after their flight.

[1] Bryant, "Dissertation on the Trojan War," p. 18.

[2] "Growth of the Homeric Poems," p. 115.

[3] Or Râvaṇ.

13. Achilles with a mighty shout daunts the whole of the Trojan army. Hanuman with a mighty shout daunts the whole of the army of Râvaṇa.

14. M. Fauche notifies one very important similarity:

Often showers of blood, an awful portent, fall from the sky in the 'Râmâyaṇa.' In the 'Iliad' on two occasions, Zeus distils in the clouds, as a sinister warning, similar showers. One of these is when the favourite son of Zeus, Sarpedon, is about to die, and Zeus and Hera are looking on unseen:

> "She said: 'The cloud compeller overcome
> Assents to Fate and ratifies the doom.
> Then touched with grief the weeping heavens distilled
> A shower of blood on all the fatal field.'"

The heavens rain blood in the "Râmâyaṇa" when the portents announce the coming death of Râvaṇa, Khara, etc.

15. The Hindu besiegers fare badly in an early fight, and Râma proposes to bring the army back to India. The Greek besiegers fare badly in an early fight, and Agamemnon proposes to carry the army back to Greece.

16. The Râkshasas (demons) of the Indian epic are as big as mountains; but Mars when thrown down by angry Pallas, who flings a rock at him, covers seven acres with his gigantic body.

17. In India the gods and demons gather round to watch the crucial battle between the paramount chiefs Râma and Râvaṇa. In the "Iliad" the opposing gods also crowd round, though the chiefs are not paramount and the encounter not crucial:

> "The gazing gods lean forward from the sky."

18. In the "Râmâyaṇa" Kuvera, the God of Gold and worldly glitter, and Śiva, the God of Death, throw dice. In the "Iliad" Jove suspends golden scales.

19. Importance is attached, as in the "Iliad," to the obsequies of the dead hero, which the generous Râma makes splendid enough.

20. Râma and Menelaus regain and carry back their wives.

21. When Sîtâ has determined to starve herself to death in Lankâ, Indra in person

comes down and gives her the Amṛita, the immortal food. Jove, when Achilles is also of the same determination, sends down Minerva with the ambrosia.

22. There are very strange points of contact between Vibhîshaṇa and Homer's Antenor. Of themselves they seem almost enough to settle the question of Indian derivation.

(1) Vibhîshaṇa is the wisest denizen in Laṅkâ Antenor has the same reputation in Troy:

> "And next the wisest of the reverend throng
> Antenor grave, and sage Eucalydon."

(2) When Râvaṇa is about to kill the ambassador Hanuman, Vibhîshaṇa remonstrates and saves his life. When Menelaus and Odysseus came into Troy to treat, they would have been killed but for the intervention of Antenor. (3) Vibhîshaṇa, inspired by the Queen-Mother, advises Râvaṇa to give up Sîtâ. Antenor advises Paris to give up Helen. (4) Antenor plots secretly against his own side, and advises Ulysses to seize the Trojan Palladium, and make the wooden

horse. The fate of Lankâ is in the hands of Vibhîshaṇa three times. When the Monkey armies and their chiefs are brought up by the sea, Vibhîshaṇa shows them how to pass it by a sacrifice to the gods, and by frightening all the sharks and sea-monsters with a taste of Râma's arrows. The attack on the Chaitya of Nikumbhila is the second advantage that they gain from the superior local knowledge of the giant. And when Indra sends down his special chariot, with the celebrated charioteer Mâtali, the Hindu princes are afraid of accepting until Vibîshaṇa assures them that it is not a snare. (5) Vibhîshaṇa, after the capture of the city, and the death of his brother, is crowned King of Lankâ. Antenor, according to Smith's "Dictionary of Greek Mythology," "founded a new kingdom of Troy out of the ruins of the old."

23. The great rocks thrown about in the "Iliad," as well as in the Indian fable, let in a flood of light. In India they are used only by the supernatural beings, who might

perhaps fling about stones as big as a four-wheeled cab. In the "Iliad," Hector smashes down a huge city gateway, strengthened with iron bars, rampart and all, with one rock; and Ajax flings another that no other athlete could lift:

> "He poised and swung it round; then, tossed on high
> It flew with force and laboured up the sky,
> Full on the Lycian's helmet thundering down,
> The ponderous ruin crushed his battered crown."

But all these analogies are nothing to what follows. The monster Râvaṇa is protected by mighty spells. He cannot be killed by a god. He has ten heads; and when one is knocked off another appears. He has only one vulnerable point in his body, the navel; and this can only be harmed by a special weapon, the Brahmaśiras. To meet these difficulties a special mortal is trained from early youth—namely, Râma. He is armed for the encounter. He has a magical body-coat, bracelets, a sword, and a bow and quiver, all constructed by Viśva-Karma, the Indian Vulcan. He has lent to him for this special encounter the famous chariot of Indra, the Supreme God, with its immortal steeds; and Mâtali, the famous charioteer.

All this figures in Homer, but in a very topsy-turvy manner, owing to the jumble between the two narratives, the Story of Menelaus and the Story of Achilles. The latter coming second into the field has made certain arbitrary borrowings.

1. We have the invulnerable fighting man, but instead of its being the arch enemy as in the Indian story, it is the avenging hero, Achilles, whose heel was dipped in the Styx. Instead of his slaughtering that foe, that foe slaughtered him.

2. He has given to him the magical body-coat and arms fresh from the anvils of the Greek Vulcan. He has a chariot lent him, with the steeds of Jove. He has the charioteer, Automedon, who alone can drive such steeds. And yet with all these preparations he fails to slay the ravisher, or to take his city. And one very important gift he has not got—the Brahmaśiras—the terrible arrow of Philoctetes, by

which alone the ravisher of Helen can be slaughtered. What this really means will, I think, be better understood if we turn first to a remarkable work, "The Rise of the Greek Epic," by Mr. Gilbert Murray. He holds that the "Iliad" was written a long time before the "Odyssey"; and that both are by many writers, having undergone much revision and alteration, in the struggle of "Hellenism" against "Paganism." "The Civilizers" have plainly attempted to efface such savage customs as slavery, subjection of women, immorality, and cruelty, and poisoned arrows. Hector's body was dragged round Troy whilst he was yet alive. Mr. Murray proves this from the "Ajax" of Sophocles and also from the "Andromache" of Euripides. And he holds that the tragedies were written after the Homeric poems, but before the "Civilizers" had got to work. This suggestion is of immense importance to our inquiry, for the "Arrow of Philoctetes" is the crux of the Homeric problems. The story is told at length in one of the tragedies of Sophocles. In obedience to the Oracle, Ulysses and

Diomedes go off to fetch Philoctetes and his bow, as it is known that Paris cannot be killed with any other weapon. The "Odyssey," coming after the "Iliad," virtually confirms the story. "Alone Philoctetes in the Trojan land surpassed me with the bow, in our Achæan archery,"[1] says Ulysses. He could not have done this unless he had come eventually to Troy. He was one of the Suitors of Helen; and the Iliad tells us why he could not come with the others.[2]

If we accept the story of Philoctetes as told by Sophocles we can put together two pictures which certainly tell a great deal. In the first the supremacy of Heaven is threatened by a mighty demon, and the great

[1] Butcher and Lang, "Odyssey" (trans.).

[2] "The troops
With Philoctetes sailed, whose matchless art
From the tough bow directs the feathered dart:
Seven were his ships; each vessel fifty row,
Skilled in his science of the dart and bow.
But he lay raging in the Lemnian ground.
A poisonous Hydra gave the burning wound;
There groaned the chief in agonizing pain,
Whom Greece at length shall wish nor wish in vain."

Destiny (or Daivan) that was believed to overrule gods, as well as men, has settled that only a man can conquer the demon giants, that are assailing Heaven. In consequence, a young hero is selected for the task by the Supreme God. He is furnished with three potent spells, which may be said to constitute only one spell, as they have to be used together.

1. The chariot, belonging to the Supreme God, has been lent to him, as I have pointed out.

2. The celestial horses of the Supreme have been lent to draw that chariot, together with the celestial charioteer, Mâtali.

3. The terrible missile called the "Brahmasiras," which alone can wound the leader of the fiends, is also lent. It is only by these three spells, one helping the other, that the terrible demon can be overcome.

The selected hero marches across India with an army. His wife has been carried off by the demon. To rescue her and punish the foul fiend, he uses the three potent spells, and the demon is killed.

Let us place by the side of this the second picture:

Olympus, the Heaven of the Greeks, has been menaced by a similar uprising of hostile and powerful giants, but that has nothing to do with the second story. The battles are all over before that story begins. A Greek lady is carried away like the Indian lady, but by a fop and not a fiend. A young hero is selected for the task of punishing this ravisher. He is furnished with three potent spells, which may be said really to constitute only one spell, as they have to be used together to be efficient.

1. The chariot belonging to the Supreme God is lent for the occasion.

2. The "deathless horses" are lent to draw that chariot, and a celestial charioteer who alone can guide those horses.

3. A terrible arrow called the "Arrow of Philoctetes," by which, when shot from the special chariot, the spell-protected ravisher can alone be slain, must also have been an item in the original story.

Now what occurred?

Two of these superhuman spells went with an expedition to the city of the ravisher; but Philoctetes and his arrow could not be brought with them. He was suffering with a wound so cruel that he had to be left behind. If we may believe Homer the army were aware of this crucial misadventure before they disembarked.[1]

Thus, for nine years and ten months the Greeks battled without any hope of victory, for each well knew that, without Philoctetes, Paris was invulnerable.

Then the Supreme God who had provided the three spells for the victory of the Greeks, and the punishment of the ravisher of his daughter, suddenly seemed to forget on which side he was fighting, and took the part of rape and plunder, with the strange result that his favourite son was killed with the magic spells.

If we are asked which was the original sketch of the story and which the copy, which one would we select?

[1] "Yet thought they on him at his ship" (Chapman). "Yet were the Argives soon to bethink them beside their ships of King Philoctetes" (Messrs. Lang and Leaf).

CHAPTER II

THE STORY OF ACHILLES

WORKMANSHIP and choosing a plot are two distinct efforts. Very little may be made of an excellent plot, and much of a very bad one. The plot, for instance, of the "Merchant of Venice," with the impossible decision of the Judge, is quite silly, but from it has emerged the best play, of the romantic drama pattern, in the world. The reader must reflect that if the plot of the story of Achilles is deficient, the great success proves that the workmanship must have been all the more extraordinary.

What is the chief *motif*—the central idea formed in the mind of the poet—in constructing this story? Plainly this: he was going to paint a hero so terrific that even his corslet, his greaves, his shield and his terrible horsehair crest had power to put to flight an army of 50,000 men. This fine *coup de théâtre* would of course be very much enhanced if the operation was conducted by a dummy; so Patroclus is depicted as a mere "squire." He lights the fires, roasts the chine, serves out the wine, escorts slave girls from the tent of one chief to that of another.

But there are many difficulties in the way. The formidable Paris, who could only be slain by a special arrow, had to be turned into a milksop in order to make way for Hector, expressly created for the opponent of Achilles. Menelaus had also to be pushed into the background. Much else had to be dislocated, as we have already seen. How old was Achilles? Certainly the Achilles of the "Iliad" is a stripling who sails to Troy as a mere boy, and, according to many prophecies, is to die very young; and the Achilles of the "Odyssey" must have been about fifty years old.

How can that be proved? In this way—his son Neoptolemus was at least twenty when he sailed in the ship of Ulysses for

Troy. Twenty added to the ten years of Troy warfare makes thirty. Supposing Achilles was fifteen years of age when he begot him, this would make Achilles forty-five.

But the expedition to Troy was made up of the unsuccessful competitors for Helen at the jousts. They had all sworn to help the successful candidate if any harm was done to Helen. Such a vast expedition could not be started in a day. It consisted, according to the calculations of Mr. Bryant, of 1,186 ships. We learn from the play, "Iphigenia in Aulis," that it took ten years to start it. Ulysses was one of these competitors. And if Neoptolemus, as the "Odyssey" affirms, took his part in the earliest battles and councils, he could not have then been a mere boy. He must have had an initiation of several years under Ulysses. Patroclus, even after nine years of Troy campaigning, was still a "squire," not a chief.

Now without doubt in the "Achilleis"—that is, the story of the "Wrath of Achilles," as distinguished from the "Ilias," or general account of the war—there is a steady attempt to make Achilles quite a young man.

Says old Phoinix to him: "To thee did the old knight Peleus send me the day he sent thee to Agamemnon forth from Phthia, a stripling yet unskilled in equal war and in debate wherein men wax pre-eminent."[1]

And we learn that Achilles was younger than Patroclus, but the latter, though very youthful, had a sort of roving commission to speak "words of wisdom"[2] to his young friend.

Then, sad on the lonely shore, Achilles thus addresses the "stormy main":

> "O parent goddess! Since in early bloom
> Thy son must fall, by too severe a doom;
> Since to so short a race of glory born,
> Great Jove in justice should this span adorn," etc.

Thetis makes the the same lament:

> "Why have I borne thee with a mother's throes,
> To Fates averse, and nursed for future woes?
> So short a space the light of heaven to view!
> So short a space! and filled with sorrow too!"

---

[1] Lang, Leaf, and Myers, "Iliad," IX. (trans.).
[2] *Ibid.*, XI.

Here also is her prayer to Zeus:

> "Fame is at least by heavenly promise due
> To life so short, and now dishonour'd too.
> Avenge this wrong, O ever just and wise!
> Let Greece be humbled and the Trojans rise."

But in these rejuvenating efforts another expedient is adopted. Homer tries to show indirectly that Achilles was not one of the suitors that were worsted when Menelaus won Helen at the jousts.

I will borrow from Professor Jebb a condensed account of what I call "The Story of Achilles":

"For ten years they (the Greeks) besieged Troy in vain, though the Trojans dared not come out and fight pitched battles; for there was a hero in the Greek army so terrible that not even Hector, the greatest of Trojan warriors, could stand before him. This hero was Achilles . . . . but at last, in the tenth year of the siege, Achilles suffered a grievous affront from the king Agamemnon, who took away from him his prize, the captive damsel, Brisêis. Then Achilles was angry, and said that he would fight for the Greeks no more. . . . The first result of Achilles refusing to fight was that the Trojans now dared to come forth and give battle to the Greeks.[1]

"The Greeks," pursues the Professor, "are hard pressed. . . . Still Achilles will not fight. But he lends his armour to Patroclus," and the death of this warrior rouses him to revenge at last.

"He rushes to the field, drives the Trojans within their walls, and slays Hector, the last hope of Troy. . . . The 'Iliad' ends with King Priam coming to ask the body of his slain son from Achilles."

There are three days' battles recorded in Homer: but if this account of Professor Jebb be correct, for the first nine and a half years of the war there was no Seige of Troy, but, to use military language, only a blockade; a blockade by one man, the terrible Achilles.

But if there was no fighting done by the banded suitors of Helen, how did Achilles become so terrible?

Says Professor Jebb:

"Helen had been wooed by many suitors, and her father Tyndareus had bound them

[1] Jebb, "Greek Literature," p. 21.

GREEK GALLEY. (*p.* 7)

RÂVANA (*p.* 105)

FIGHT FOR THE BODY OF PATROCLUS. (*p.* 24)

Face p. 24

all by an oath to join in avenging that man whom she should marry, if she were taken from him by force."

Now the catalogue of the ships in the "Iliad" places Achilles, in its records, as one of these suitors. And this catalogue belongs to the earliest part of the "Iliad"—that which we call the Story of Menelaus. He is said, moreover, to have sailed with Agamemnon. His ships were brought up with the others for the long stay at Aulis; and his name was there used to induce the mother of poor Iphigenia to send her daughter up to be sacrificed to obtain a favourable wind. She arrived to be, as she thought, the bride of Achilles.

Professors are naturally more at home with the arts of peace than the arts of slaughter, but anyone who has seen real war could have told Professor Jebb that the Achilles of Homer, if he was a suitor—that is, a subordinate officer of King Agamemnon—would have disorganized any army in a month. Take his proclamation of a truce of twelve days, and see how it would work. Let us suppose that a body of light troops belonging to the Greek army was confronted with a body of light troops of the enemy near the Trimulus of Ilus. The Greek commander, say, advances and shouts out: "Ho there! Achilles has ordered a twelve days' truce." The Trojan commander would certainly say to himself, "Achilles! A paltry captain! This must be treachery!" And he would probably let fly a shower of arrows at the conciliating Greek. Similar bewilderment would be in the minds of the Greeks when they were informed; and for a long time neither side would know whether it was peace or war. With Agamemnon the case would be much more serious. If he supported Achilles he would confess himself superseded in the command ever afterwards. Plainly, he would have to string up that turbulent officer to a bough, say, of the beech tree at the Scæan gate. What force could take the field if every swashbuckler attached to it thought he had the right to "convene" a general assembly, and heap ferocious epithets upon his Commander-in-Chief every time a fortune-teller told him a yarn? And how could he "convene" his meeting, if the heralds and staff obeyed that Commander-in-Chief alone? Even early Greek discipline would teach that to raise your hand against your Commander, and dictate to him what camp followers he may punish and what he must let alone, is scarcely orthodox soldiery. The fate of Thersites, and of Ulysses when he shammed madness and began to plough the seashore, show plainly enough that the Greek Commanders were not so very forebearing. And even the blustering words of Achilles were not authenticated by deeds. He gave up Brisêis to Agamemnon.

Other parts of Professor Jebb's analysis seem to fade away.

1. There are three days' battles recorded in Homer, and the "terrible Achilles" never drew his sword before Troy at all, until the thirtieth day of the tenth year, the day of the third of the three battles.

2. In the earliest version of the "Iliad," the Story of Menelaus, the two first battles went

completely to the Greeks, the Trojans on each occasion being driven to the city gates.

3. The truce of twelve days, if it existed, certainly did not end the war. The Greeks, by oath, were banded together to punish the ravisher of Helen. No attempt was made by Achilles to do that. Instead, Paris killed him.

4. Hector is a dummy. He is ignored even in the "Odyssey."

5. Professor Gilbert Murray points out that in an earlier account of Troy, the "Cypria," Calchas figures already; and is mixed up in a more woeful tragedy.

It is a strange fact that in the Homeric poems, poor Iphigenia, and all the characters of the most pathetic story of early Greece, are present on the stage; but the catastrophe, her death, has been sponged completely out to give place to a blustering swashbuckler. We have Iphigenia, Agamemnon, Clytemnestra, Orestes, Diana, Achilles the lover, and Calchas at Aulis outpouring Diana's anger.

Mr. Bryant, in his "Dissertation on the

Trojan War," remarks that it is a very odd thing that Achilles alone would seem to have moved about during the whole ten years' war. The other forces, winter as well as summer, seemed glued to the spot, with no communication at all from the outside world. Agamemnon confesses that "the timber of the ships was quite decayed and the rigging quite loose." There is no mention of recruits, repairs, revictualment. Phthia is only three days' sail from Troy, and yet Achilles does not know whether his father is alive or dead.

"For I should think, that my father Peleus is either absolutely dead, or barely alive: and under the last afflictions of old age."[1]

But this suggests an important question. Why was Achilles the only chief allowed to go cruising about? He sacks twelve cities from shipboard and eleven by land expeditions —Lesbos, Tenedos, Lyrnissos, Scyros, Thebe, are mentioned. It was intended indirectly to show that Achilles at Troy was

[1] Bryant, "Dissertation of the Trojan War," p. 28.

on a different footing from that of the other chieftains, who were bound by a solemn oath by Menelaus to remain fighting until Troy fell.

But does all this really prove Achilles to have been a very young man?

Take Scyros. If Achilles really sacked that city and made the mother of Neoptolemus, the Princess Deidameia, pregnant he must have made his expedition there several years before Helen's rape. Otherwise his son Neoptolemus could only have been a boy of eight or nine years old when he lectured the generals in camp upon the art of war. Certainly it would throw back the sea and land expeditions of Achilles indefinitely. For instance, at Thebe, he killed King Eetion and his seven sons, and he captured Queen Astynome, the King's wife, who figured afterwards as Chryseis. But according to this date he must have done this some fifteen odd years before the rape of Helen.

Queen Astynome is a puzzle. She was a grandmother when the fuss was made about her. She was a buxom widow, the mother of seven sons and one daughter, when first carried off by Achilles. That daughter must have been already married to Hector and lodged in Troy before the Greeks arrived and blockaded the city. That would make her about twenty-seven years of age, and her mother certainly over fifty. But the language of some of the characters who figured in the turbulent scene when the "Iliad" opens, shows that quite a different view of Queen Astynome also prevailed.

Says Agamemnon:

> "Because my prize, my beauteous maid, I hold,
> And heavenly charms prefer to proffer'd gold.
> A maid, unmatch'd in manners as in face,
> Skill'd in each art, and crown'd with every grace;
> Not half so dear were Clytæmnestra's charms,
> When first her blooming beauties bless'd my arms."

Now this is certainly not the language of a sedate chief talking about a lady, a grandmother, of fifty years of age. And the inspired priest Calchas, who knew all the objective details of the case, could scarcely have called Astynome the "black-eyed maid," and said that it was Agamemnon who "provoked the raging pest," if the presence of the lady was due to the siege of Thebe.

And what about the desolate picture of the snivelling priest Chryses, wandering "by the sounding main," and crying: "Oh, give Chryseis to these arms again"?[1]

It is plain that the fiction of a ten years' war, if not invented for Achilles, has been specially utilized in his favour. The contradictions that emerge from the two conflicting narratives are pushed up to a pinnacle of unreason at this point. According to Grote, the Greek army mounted to 100,000 men. Those of Achilles are roughly computed at 2,750 men, as we have seen. And yet we

[1] Messrs. Lang, Leaf, and Myers call her a "child," but the difficulty is a great deal more than verbal. Chrysa was plainly a sea-port, as Chryseis was taken back there in a ship by Ulysses, and presented to her father with much pomp. If Chryses was a priest of the great Temple of Apollo at Chrysa, for at least twenty-seven years he must have been almost entirely separated from his daughter, Queen Astynome, for Thebe is forty miles from the sea. Would he call an Imperial lady of fifty years of age a "child"? Why, too, did he foregather with Achilles to help him—Achilles who had just barbarously slaughtered his seven grandsons?

are called upon to believe that Achilles during the first nine years of the war carried away these men for his twelve land and eleven sea campaigns; and that the remaining 97,000 odd warriors remained inactive in front of Troy. A minor absurdity here would be that not one of these heroes was even trying to fulfil his solemn oath, which was to kill Paris for his great crime. The stout Greeks under Agamemnon were only blockading him; and Achilles was slaughtering crowds of people who most probably did not know that Helen existed. Does not this raise many questions? Why were ten years of war necessary? "Smith's Dictionary" shows that Helen was first carried away by Theseus; and that her brothers, Castor and Pollux, went to Athens and rescued her without delaying nine years, or even one. This fits much more closely into the story of Râma, who, with his brother, Lakshmaṇa, are called in the "Râmâyaṇa" the Asvins, or Twins, of the Indian Zodiac. Another early legend noticed in "Smith's Dictionary" is that Helen was for some time in the power of Proteus. Here we get Kâma-rûpa, a nickname of Râvaṇa—the "demon who changes his form at will." Then Helen telling King Priam the names of the Greek warriors at the beginning of the tenth year, seems to show that he could not have watched them for nine previous years. Would a study of the Indian "Râmâyaṇa" throw a light on these puzzles, that a study of the Homeric poems renders difficult enough? What if a bold improvisatore like Demodocus had composed a version of Râma's story, the "Fall of Thebe"? Râma, to avenge Sîtâ, whom he believes to have been defiled by Râvaṇa, the Master of Laṅkâ slaughters him, his three brothers, Khara, Dûshan and Kumbhakarna, and his sons Aksha and Indrajit. Achilles, though King Eetion has never wronged him at all, is made to imitate this wholesale butchery on the King and his seven sons. Achilles says that this capture of Thebe was more difficult than the siege of Troy.[1]

[1] The spot usually fixed as the site of Troy is a plain, marshy in many places, decorated with tamarisk bushes,

Homeric poems were at first the recitation sketches of Demodocus and Phemius; short, telling, confined to one sitting. Also they had a money value, and as such were kept private. Homer, says Mr. Gilbert Murray, left the "Cypria," as his daughter's dowry, and the "Taking of Oechalia," to his heir, Creophylus.[1] Our suggested sketch, the "Taking of Thebe," fulfils these conditions. Thebe had to be substituted for Troy, as an equivalent for Laṅkâ. And Homer on other points showed a partiality for strong effects. Had Vâlmîki's picture of Râvaṇa anything to do with Homer's picture of Zeus? Both potentates are on the side of rape, outrage, robbery. Both by miraculous means slaughter

---

and girt by the rocky spurs and the more distant highlands of the Ida range. Achilles had under him 2,750 men. Did his trip to Thebe and his other land expeditions start from this plain? If so, how far would the forces have got, starting without carriage, without portable food, without tents, and led by a raw youth who knew nothing of war? Thebe is some forty miles inland. It must be more difficult under such circumstances tc take Thebe than to take Troy.

[1] "Rise of the Greek Epic," p. 93.

the besiegers in thousands, Zeus by guiding the arrows of the Trojans, Râvaṇa by sending serpentine arrows, which move about of their own accord, killing everybody. Both produce dense darkness at midday; and mists that specially save Indrajit, who, according to Monsieur Fauche, as I have shown, figures in Troy as Hector. Both rain blood as portents when their sons are about to die.

But I have not yet done with Râvaṇa. He had two aspects—a necessity if he were Síva. Was the picture of Hector the better side of Râvaṇa? The grief of Mandodarî, Râvaṇa's wife, is very pathetic; and reminds one of the grief of the parting of Hector and Andromache, transforming it from a "lament" into a dramatic scene. There are three characters in each — the most illustrious warrior in the defence of the City of Transgression; an exceptionally noble woman, his wife; and their little son. Both wives urge their husbands not to fight, the Indian matron taking the high ground that the war is unjust. Both have a premonition of disaster. And the poem of Vâlmîki strikes the deepest note of woe, because widowhood and the scorn and servitude that come to the wives of defeated soldiers are already the lot of the lady, in fact and not in surmise. Homer's effort is considered the gem of the "Iliad," and it is very touching:

LAMENT OF MANDODARÎ.

His sleep is sound
Who had a god for brother, God of Gold;
And on the ground
He lies by broken cars and corpses cold;
The piteous screams of widows that deplore him
Make sad the night,
The God that holds the Vajra quailed before him
In awful fight.
Oh, where is now the bow
That laid whole cohorts low,
And made the God of Light
A conqueror to know?

I counselled thee to shun this fateful war,
O spouse esteemed!
A woman's love scents peril from afar,
By man undreamed.
I saw thy fate advancing from the plain,
I saw thy fate advancing through the main—
And thou wert told,

By thine own brother Vîbishaṇa sage,
To still fierce Râma's rage
By giving back his wife;
Nor in the balance place
In the one scale thy soul, thy realm, thy life—
And in the next success that meant disgrace.

Thy wife why didst thou scorn?
From Mâyâ goddess in the eternal spheres
That wife was born.
Mâyâ! Illusion! was her name!
In the bright heavens she distanced all compeers—
Illusion was her fame.
The gods they clustered round her as the bees
Seek the illusion of the honeyed trees;
And when in heaven's groves
In famed Kailâs we plucked the asphodels,
Thou and thy bride,
And wandered side by side,
Thou saidst to me that Mâyâ's spells
Nourished our loves.

Black night it comes to all—
In my swift car that glistened like the sun,
And stole its hue,
I wandered through the realms my spouse had won,
Shaturnijetri at my side,
Our infant boy and pride,
And with his father true.
Great King, take up once more thy broken lance,
Thy breastplate torn,

Trust all again to fickle battle's chance
And save thy wife from scorn
And servitude, and many days of pain.
Answer, O King, thy wife forlorn !
I call to thee in vain.

The gods are watchful and the gods are just,
They fling the malefactor in the dust;
And in thine eyes,
Sîtâ could place a balm, a salve amazing.
It conjured up a thousand ecstasies,
Dreams without substance, glamours that were dazing;
For Sîtâ's balm
It brought no calm,
Its name was Death.

It is difficult to read this without thinking of the touching scenes between Hector and Andromache, also accompanied by a little boy.

The farewells in the "Iliad" have other points of analogy :

MANDODARÎ.

Great Prince, it is not wise for thee to confront great Râma,

O chief do not cause the ruin of this city. Do not offer up thine entire family.

ANDROMACHE.

Too daring prince, ah! whither dost thou run?
Ah! too forgetful of thy wife and son.
Greece in her single heroes strove in vain—
New hosts oppose thee and thou must be slain.

The Prowess of the Chief Enemy.

Râma, the son of Daśaratha is more than man. He killed thy brother Khara, and routed his hordes. There, too, he killed Inciras Kabandha and Virâdha, and broke to pieces all the hosts of Bali. The Janasthâna reeks with slaughtered foes, thy faithful soldiers. My fears began when he pierced Mârîcha in the Daṇḍaka wood. He had gone there as an anchorite, bound by a vow of his father. Oh, why hast thou brought him away?

The fierce Achilles wrapt our walls in fire,
Laid Thebe waste, and slew my warlike sire;
His fate compassion in the victor bred,
Stern as he was, he yet revered the dead.
By the same arm my seven brave brothers fell,
In one sad day beheld the gates of hell.
My mother lived to wear the victor's bands,
The Queen of Hippodacia's sylvan lands.
Redeemed too late, she scarce beheld again
Her pleasing empire and her native plain,
When, ah! oppressed by life consuming woe
She fell a victim to Diana's bow.

Three Sorties.

Three times bold chiefs have led thy multitudes beyond the city walls.

Thrice our bold foes the fierce attack have given.

THE MEETING OF HECTOR AND ANDROMACHE (*p.* 39)

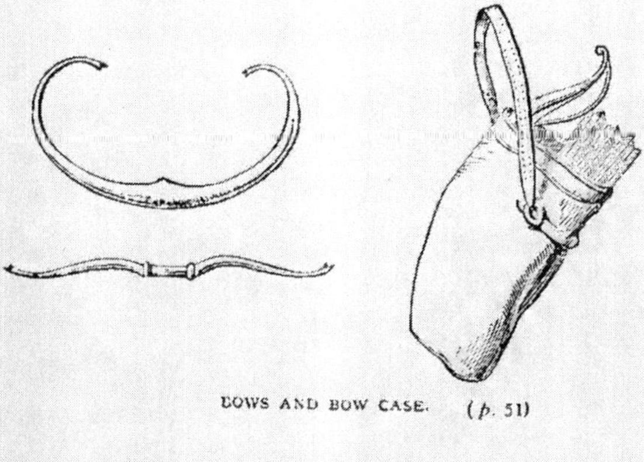

BOWS AND BOW CASE. (*p.* 51)

[Face

More Lives than One threatened.

Thus speaks thy wife, Thy city, and thy kin, In thee are centred all.	Whilst yet my Hector still survives I see My father, mother, brethren, all in thee.
RÂVAṆA.	HECTOR.
Thy speech, sweet Queen, cannot be considered. What would be my life if shorn of its splendour? I have robbed the son of Daśaratha of his wife, and basely boasted of it. I have brought vast armies to defend my capital. My victories have been over gods and demons. I have routed Indra and the Immortals.	Andromache, my soul's far better part, Why with untimely sorrows heave thy heart? No hostile hand can antedate my doom, Till fate condemns me to the silent tomb. How would the souls of Troy in arms renowned, And Troy's proud dames, whose garments sweep the ground, Attaint the lustre of my former name, Should Hector basely quit the field of fame?

Both Heroes have Premonitions.

I know that Râma slaughtered Madhu. I know that I must perish at his hand, but I shall not make peace with him.	Yet come it will the day decreed by Fates. How my heart trembles, whilst my tongue relates— The day when thou imperial Troy must bend, And see thy warriors fall, thy glories end.

CHAPTER III

STORY OF ULYSSES

THE "Odyssey" is usually described as a continuation of the "Iliad"; but this is plainly not the case, as the four opening lines testify:

> "The Man for wisdom's various arts renowned,
> Long exercised in woes, O Muse! resound;
> Who when his arms had wrought the destined fall
> Of sacred Troy and razed her heaven-built wall."

The poet evidently here affirms that Ulysses captured Troy. He it was whose cunning art devised the wooden horse, and who stole the Palladium. This story puts aside Achilles altogether. Menelaus, asked which was the greatest hero in the war, answers thus:

"For them all I make no such dole, despite my grief, as for one only, who causes me to loathe both sleep and meat, when I think upon him. For no one of the Achæans toiled so greatly as Odysseus toiled and adventured himself."[1]

Would anyone judge that Achilles was the one stupendous character in the Trojan War from this speech?

Here is the second speech of Menelaus:

"Ere now have I learned the counsel and the thought of many heroes, and travelled over many a land, but never yet have mine eyes beheld any such man of heart as was Odysseus."[2]

In point of fact the "Odyssey" seems a complete story of an Aryan Sun-hero like Râma, with the order a little dislocated. He wins the bride of a Svayaṁvara, but as it was notorious that this was not Helen, he is obliged to postpone this fact to the end of his story. He has more than his share of the usual fateful "banishment." He goes to Troy, and is there chief hero. Like Râma, he is tempted by a witch with exquisite supposititious charms. He succumbs for seven

[1] Butcher and Lang, "Odyssey," IV. 51 (trans.).
[2] *Ibid.*, 56.

years. He visits hell like Râma. His wife, a noble creation, and much nearer to the Indian heroine than other Homeric women, is surrounded by a foul band of "suitors," as they are called; and they seek to destroy her purity, like the Râkshasas of Lańkâ, by whom they were probably suggested.

The descent into hell seems put in on purpose to get rid of Achilles altogether.

We learn that at the siege of Troy there was a hero named Neoptolemus, who rivalled his father Achilles in valour. He slew "hosts" of Trojans, and was the only hero in the wooden horse that did not quail. He went to Troy with the expedition, with Ulysses in his good hollow ship, and was in the camp ten years, and left with much spoil. He was at all the councils of war, and surpassed all except Ulysses and Nestor in wisdom and eloquence. And yet his father Achilles was not aware that he went to Troy at all.

In the "Odyssey" the shade of Achilles puts this question to Ulysses:[1]

[1] Butcher and Lang, "Odyssey," XI. p. 187 (trans.).

"But come, tell me tidings of that lordly son of mine—did he follow to the war to be a leader or not?"

This is the answer:

"Concerning thy dear son Neoptolemus, I will tell thee all the truth, according to thy word. It was I that led him up out of Scyros in my good hollow ship, in the wake of the goodly greaved Achæans. Now oft as we took counsel around Troy town, he was ever the first to speak, and no word missed the mark; the godlike Nestor and I alone surpassed him. But whensoever we Achæans did battle on the plain of Troy, he never tarried behind in the throng or the press of men, but ran far out before us all, yielding to none in that might of his. And many men he slew in warfare dread; but I could not tell of all or name their names, even all the host he slew in succouring the Argives, save only how he smote with the sword that son of Telephus, the hero Eurypylus, and many Ceteians of his company were slain around him, by reason of a woman's bribe. He truly was the comeliest man that ever I saw, next to goodly

Memnon. And again when we, the best of the Argives, were about to go down into the horse which Epeus wrought, and the charge of all was laid on me, both to open the door of our good ambush and to shut the same, then did the other princes and counsellors of the Danaans wipe away the tears, and the limbs of each one trembled beneath him, but never once did I see thy son's fair face wax pale, nor did he wipe the tears from his cheeks. . . .

After we had sacked the steep city of Priam, he embarked unscathed with his share of the spoil." [1]

Other borrowings occur :

Like Tâḍakâ, a female giant Scylla figures. She seizes half a dozen sailors and munches them up simultaneously ; and we get even more direct plagiarism in the matter of the one-eyed Cyclops, Polyphemus, who snaps up the two sailors of Ulysses in his monstrous hands. He is the mighty giant Danu, of the Indian story, also one-eyed. Danu seizes Râma and Lakshmaṇa in the same way.

[1] Butcher and Lang, "Odyssey," XI. p. 188 (trans.).

Ulysses puts out his giant's one eye. The brave Indian heroes hack off the gigantic hands of their enemy; and there is a palpable suggestion for the Sirens of the Greek work in the Indian account of the "Golden Cavern of the Five Apsaras" (Nymphs of India), with its golden trees and gem fruits. Soft songs come up from below as the rash stranger stands gazing at the enchanted lake. He is enticed into the cavern, but can never find the way out. He leaves his bones there.

Penelope, working and undoing her tapestry, is an Homeric picture that young girls love; but the satirical author of "Erewhon," Mr. Butler, views it from a different standpoint. "Let us see what the 'Odyssey' asks us to believe, or rather, to swallow," says Mr. Butler. "We are told that more than a hundred young men fell violently in love at the same time with a supposed widow, who before the close of their suit could hardly have been under forty, and who had a grown-up son—pestering her for several years with addresses that they know are most distasteful to her. They are so madly in love with her that they cannot think of proposing to anyone else till she has made her choice. When she has done this they will go; till then, they will pay her out for her cruel treatment of them by eating her son Telemachus out of house and home. This, therefore, they proceed to do, and Penelope, who is a model wife and mother, suffers agonies of grief, partly because of the death of her husband, and partly because she cannot get the suitors out of the house."[1] Mr. Butler shows also that these suitors leave the house very quietly every night, and that on one occasion Penelope threatened to forbid the return of one of them—a threat that she might have executed as often as she liked, apparently, as she was living quite close to her father-in-law, from whom Ulysses had derived the immense wealth that was now being squandered. She might have gone to him for protection. Can we find for these transactions any other interpretation than that of Mr. Butler less damaging to the talent of the author?

[1] Butler, "Authoress of the Odyssey," p. 125.

My suggestion is this: Three of the leading events in the Life of Râma have been welded into one little drama by an author whose leading idea, as I have already shown, seems to have been to give to Ulysses a zodiacal biography similar to that of Râma; or, if it be true that the "Return of Ulysses" and the "Death of the Suitors" were originally separate stories, he may have furbished up the last with jousts and archery and much bloodshed—points that he knew were popular with the audiences of Demodocus and Phemius.

In the story of Râma, Sîtâ is carried away to Lankâ by the Ten-headed Fiend. Two facts are noteworthy during her stay there: she is in the complete power of a demon King, but her honour is safe, as he hopes to kill her husband and marry her.

This is the *motif* with Penelope also. Any one of the suitors might have assaulted her in the unprotected house at night, but all behave admirably, the reason given being that each hopes to marry her and get her fortune. Then the women of Râvaṇa's palace are fiends who bully Sîtâ, and the women of Penelope are many of them no better than they should be, and the men are what would be called behind the scenes of a theatre "general utility." At first they are gay young country squires, a little too fond of drink and good cheer; then they wear the flowery wreaths of bridegrooms—would-be bridegrooms—and come forward to box and shoot with the bow, the old-world bride-groom test; thirdly, they are shut up in a room to act as easy targets to Ulysses, who, imitating Râma in the presence of Khara or Dûshaṇ, desires to show that it is quite possible for one archer to slaughter a large army.

Mr. Butler declares that this massacre of the suitors is an insoluble puzzle. Twelve axes were set up in a room by Telemachus. "First he dug a good trench and set up the axes, one long trench for them all, and over it he made straight the line and round about stamped in the earth. And amazement fell on all that beheld how orderly he set the axes, though never before had he seen it so." [1]

[1] Butcher and Lang, "Odyssey," XXI. 348 (trans.).

The setting up of the axes firmly and in a rigid line was all that Telemachus sought to do, and his success astonished him. "His perfect skill the wondrous gazers eyed." That is Pope's version. Professor Jebb tells us that after the suitors had each tried to string the great bow and failed, Ulysses strung it easily, and then sent an arrow through the twelve "helve-holes" (*helve* is an old Anglo-Saxon word for "handle"). But to execute this feat without a miracle the line of flight through the helve-holes must have been parallel with the line of the ground, whereas each helve-hole of Telemachus was at right angles to it, and the handle still in. These handles would have to be taken out and the metal adjusted and supported for the work, a mechanical feat quite beyond anybody there. Was there a miracle? The story is plainly a version of Râma's feat. To show his power to King Sugrîva he shot an arrow through the stems of seven Talipot palm-trees ranged in line But he used the "Bow of Śiva," which he won at the jousts. And to emphasize this feat, perhaps, we are told that his arrow, after splitting the tree-stems, roared along thunderously until it reached Pâtâla, Śiva's hell. Then Ulysses has one quiver of arrows. Flaxman, who knew more about ancient Greek arms than modern English ones, gives a drawing of it. You can count the arrows—about a dozen. With these he begins to slaughter over a hundred men in a room.

"Draw your blades, . . . and let us all have at him!"[1] cries Eurymachus—an unnecessary urging, for the rear of the crowd would have at once pushed the front right up to the bold archer and overwhelmed him.

The "Death of the Suitors" and the "Fall of Thebe" are little improvisatore sketches which throw light the one on the other.

[1] Butcher and Lang, "Odyssey," XXII., 361 (trans.).

CHAPTER IV

THE "RÂMÂYAṆA"

FROM the last three chapters I think that there is a strong presumption that Homer must have seen the "Râmâyaṇa" of Vâlmîki.

It is, however, only a small part of the evidence that I propose to adduce in favour of a connection between the Greek and the Indian writers. That evidence will be divided into three sections:

1. The strange analogies between Vâlmîki and Homer.

2. A connection almost as striking between the stories of Hercules and Râma. This, if established, would quite upset the theory of the Modernist Sanskrit scholars that the story of the "Iliad" is very, very much older than that of the "Siege of Lañkâ."

3. I shall show that the great Battle of

the Gods described in Hesiod, and the great Battle of the Gods described in the "Râmâyaṇa" are precisely the same; and that the Indian story alone has any historical basis.

I will begin with a digest of the great poem, pointing out here and there analogies as they arise, but striving to reproduce some of the pathos and some of the poetry of Vâlmîki's work.

The story opens with a description of the worthy King Daśaratha, monarch of Ayodhyâ, the capital of Kauśala. Daśaratha was at once King, chief warrior and chief saint, or medicine-man, like the rulers of all early savage tribes. He had practical initiation in Indian asceticism. He "was versed in the Vedas and the six Angas." His sight was as keen as that of an eagle. He was supremely just, strong and valiant. Happiness was the lot in his capital of the poor and the rich. That city was seated on the River Saryû and was girt with ramparts and tall towers. Ayodhyâ in Sanskrit means "the Impregnable City." Broad streets, filled daily with merchants and nobles and horses and elephants, skirted proud buildings, each surrounded by bowery trees. There were fountains and flowers and public gardens. There were altars for all the gods, where the sacred fire for ever burned. Lutes, flutes and tambourines made pleasant music. Priests were abundant, and soldiers with clubs and bow and *Śataghnis*, which Colonel Yule believed to have been a prehistoric rocket or torpedo. Plainly, King Daśaratha ought to have been a contented man.

But the very reverse was the case. From none of his wives could he obtain a son to succeed him. This is a crucial calamity with the early races. And more was behind: a demon named Râvaṇa, whose palace was in Laṅkâ, or Ceylon, had suddenly taken it into his evil brain to vex Upper India as well as the South. He sent forth his Râkshasas to spoil the crops, to withhold rain, to spread fever and famine; and even to vex the holy ascetics performing Yoga in the jungles. Râvaṇa was a mortal who, by his astounding mortifications and penances, had gained a great reputation for sanctity ; and by means of this he had beguiled Brahmâ, the Lord of Heaven, to give him entry into the ranks of the immortals. The god had promised that neither god nor demon should have power to kill him. Fortified by this, his mortifications had increased an hundredfold, and also his miraculous powers. Even the gods were astounded. In a body they repaired to Brahmâ :

"The rites are done, and now the gods arise
And seek the silvered mountain in the skies.
There sits the Lord of All in awful state ;
They prostrate fall and him importunate :
'Great Brahmâ, Judge of every mortal deed,
A misplaced favour thou didst once concede,
By rites austere and semblance of a saint,
False Râvaṇ mimed a life without a taint.'
"O grant me, Lord," he cried, "in days of strife
That god or demon ne'er shall take my life!"
Thou didst consent. He joined the bands of hell
And all thy hosts are palsied by this spell ;
The gods he daunts—he frightens every one—
Indra himself was vanquished by his son ;
The Hotris fear to tend the sacred fire,
All hushed the music of the heavenly quire ;
The fruitful sun no longer gilds the land,
No more the wavelets tumble on the strand !

> Give ear, O Lord of Wisdom, Lord of Power!
> Tis thine alone to save us in the hour!
> Tis thine to baffle quibble and deceit,
> And smite the culprit with a vengeance fleet;
> A calm astounding—fateful—everywhere—
> Like brooding thunder taints the waveless air.' "

The Creator of the Universe paused for a moment or two, and then pronounced these words: " I promised that no god or no evil spirit should ever kill Râvaṇa. But I said nothing about men. By man Râvaṇa can be killed."

These words comforted the gods; and they looked round the world for a fitting hero, and their glance fell on Daśaratha, who was about to celebrate a horse-sacrifice (*aswamédha*) to obtain a long-desired son. Was there not a superstition in those days that the horse-sacrifice was the most potent of spells?

This gives the Battle of the Gods, which is the story of the "Râmâyaṇa." Had it any historical basis? The question is answered both by the Eastern Aryans and the Eranians. The "Râmâyaṇa" states that Bali or Śiva, by ascetic practices, attained so much magical power that he remained Master of the Three Worlds. That means that the religion of Śiva overcame the polytheism of the early Aryans. Bali conquers Indra. Râvaṇa conquers Indra. Râvaṇa's son, Indrajit, is named the "Conqueror of Indra" by the Supreme Brahmâ. A passage in the "Râmâyaṇa" specially describes Râvaṇa as having "overthrown the thirty-three gods of Vedism and defeated even the Monarch of the Immortals."[1]

Turning to the "Zend Avesta," the earliest record of the Western Aryans, we find strong anathemas and excommunications levelled against their brethren in India for having adopted the religion of the Devas. Anra Mainyas, better known as Ahriman, is the "Deva of Devas"—that is, Śiva. The name Shiva is actually used: "I combat Shauru."[2] All Persian scholars affirm that this is Śiva under his name "Shaurva." Professor Spiegel shows that

[1] Fauche, "Râmâyaṇa."

[2] "Fargard," x., ver. 17.

the name "Shauru" is also in the "Bundehesh."[1]

This, in a few words, is what occurred in Greece :

Ouranos had for wife Gæa, Mother Earth. From her were born Kronos, Hyperion, Briareus, Gyges, Cotta and a number of other sons, whom the father called Titans and shut up in the bowels of the earth. This caused these Titans to conspire with their mother against their father. Armed with a scythe, Kronos boldly attacked him, and treated him as Typhon treated the body of Osiris, and usurped his position as the god of gods. Titanus, the elder brother of Kronos, assisted him in all this and allowed Kronos the sovereignty of the spheres on condition that he raised no male children. Kronos, to fulfil this contract, ate up his children one by one, to the grief of their mother Rhœa. When Zeus was born, that lady secreted him, and gave her husband a stone wrapped up in a cloth. This he greedily swallowed. Zeus was concealed in

[1] "Avesta," vol. ii., p. 29.

a cave on Mount Ida in Crete. When he grew up he released his brothers. Kronos disgorged them, including the big stone. But Zeus, suspecting that his father had a design to murder him, having first of all fought for his father, afterwards attacked and deposed him.

Here, in brief, we have the historical story of the "Râmâyaṇa:"—Kronos or Śiva dethrones Ouranos or Indra. Then Zeus or Brahmâ dethrones Kronos and his crew.

All this is vital; but not to interrupt the narrative too much I will take it up afterwards.

The gods, having selected their human champion, debated in council how to help him:

"Said Brahmâ to the gods assembled there,
'For this great fight we must in time prepare;
Ten-headed Râvaṇ, with his foul intrigue
And magic spells, has formed a monstrous league.
The gods have set a mortal in the front,
'Tis meet we help him in the battle's brunt;
Let all beget fit warriors for the wars—
Sons of Gandharves, Apsaras, and Kinnars—
Spread demi-gods in every fruitful womb,
To march with Râma in the day of doom,
Each hero an immortal, as is meet,

A Deva nourished in the gods' Amṛit.[1]
Supernal bears the leafy shades to fill;
And wondrous Vanars,[2] who can change at will,
Swell out to monstrous size, and use with ease
Mountains for bolts, for clubs the tallest trees;
With shouts that match the thunder in the cloud,
Resistless, dauntless, like the lion proud'—
Such the great apes for Brahmâ's high emprise,
Their forms like mountains seemed to scale the skies."[3]

I may mention here that "Ten-Headed Râvaṇa" had this peculiarity: If one of his

[1] "Immortels qui se nourrissent d'ambroisie" (Fauche-Âdikâṇḍa, "Râmâyaṇa," XX., 3, 4 [trans.]).

[2] Monkeys.

[3] "Oui! répondent les Dieux, qui, aussitôt cette approbation donnée aux paroles de Brahma, se mettent à procréer des fils d'une vigueur égale à celle qu'ils possédaient eux-mêmes. C'étaient d'héroiques singes, capable de se métamorphoser comme ils voulaient, que ces enfants issus des Dieux, des Rishis, des Yakshas, des Gandharvas, des Siddhas et des Kinnaras. Excités par le désir d'arracher la vie à Râvaṇa, le monstre aux dix têtes, les Dieux firent naître à millier ces orangs aux formes changeantes à volonté, impétueux comme une masse de nuées orageuses, à la force sans mesure, à la voix formidable comme la bruit du tonnerre, avec le corps vigoureux des lions, la stature des éléphants ou même la hauteur des montagnes" (Fauche-Âdikâṇḍa, "Râmâyaṇa," XX. 7-10).

heads was knocked off in battle, it immediately grew again. But this latter fact and the preceding incidents bring us at once to startling coincidences. The Hydra, the potent fiend that threatened the throne of Zeus, had nine heads, and these had a peculiarity similar to those of Râvana. They also grew again immediately they were cut off. There was one exception, one head, that alone could be injured :[1] The spells of Râvaṇa, too, would not protect him if he were struck in the navel.

But a more startling incident is behind. The early mythology of Greece is based on an idea similar to that of India. There was an appalling crisis in Heaven which could only be settled by a mortal hero, a *bona fide* man. Jove was told by Minerva that the Gigantes were not invulnerable if he called a mortal hero to his assistance. In this crisis the Thunderer parented Hercules in the womb of Alcmena. Euripides tells us that Hercules with his sole arm restored to the

[1] Jacobi, "Dictionnaire Mythologique," Art. Hydra.

gods the honours that men had filched from them. Let us listen also to Hesoid:

> "But other counsel secret wove
> Within his breast the sire of gods and men—
> That both to gods and to th' inventive race
> Of man, a great deliverer might arise
> Sprung from his loins."[1]

As the story of Hercules is the earliest contribution of the Troy epic I propose to keep it in view through this little sketch of the great Indian poem.

I may mention here that the "Râmâyaṇa" has a conspicuous blemish. It has been much interpolated, and not very skilfully interpolated, by the sect called Vaishṇavas, because they worship Neo Vishṇu as the Supreme God. This sect did not come into power until after their conflict with Buddhism, from which they stole their vegetarianism and much else. Owing to these interpolations, there are two clashing accounts of the birth of Râma in the "Râmâyaṇa."[2]

[1] Hesiod, "Shield of Hercules."

[2] In the "Mahâbhârata" is a condensed account of Râma's story, and in it the hero is purely human.

The Vaishṇavas make Râma to be one of the incarnations of Vishṇu, and they have inserted a scene in which a mighty giant appears (Vishṇu probably in person) and he gives a magical potion to Kauśalyâ, Râma's mother, to drink, and portions of the magical liquor to the other queens. From this are born simultaneously Râma and Lakshmaṇa, and Bharata and Śatrughna.

The *aswamédha*, or "horse-sacrifice," is believed by scholars to have been a superstition of the ancient Scythians, brought with them to India by the Aryans, with whom for hundreds of years it was the supreme magical spell. It was a rude test of sovereignty. Like the scapegoat of the Jews, the horse was let loose, and it wandered about for a whole year supervised by armies who used it in the light of a gauntlet of defiance. With much pomp it was then killed, and the wives of the King had to pass the night by its carcase. It was the profoundest of spells. Of course, it was utterly absurd of the Vaishṇavas to turn Râma into the Supreme God when the whole point of the original story was that deliverance could only come from the hand of a man.

"From his infancy Lakhsmaṇa was attached by strong friendship to Râma, beloved of all creatures. His help was of great service to the elder brother. The just and conquering Lakhsmaṇa was dearer to Râma than his life" (chap. xix.).

Another passage throws light on this, and as, I think, I shall show by-and-by on the friendship of Agamemnon and Menelaus.

"The anchorite was followed by these two heroes, as the God of Heaven is followed by the two Aśvins" (chap. xxvi., ver. 8).

The Aśvins are the twins of the Zodiac. The boys grew quickly, and in due time were handed over to a saint, or Ṛishi, and carried by him into the solitudes of the forest to be taught the art of war, which in those days had magic and spells for prominent ingredients. The name of the Ṛishi was Viśvâmitra.

Râma went through a vigil of six nights—a more prolonged vigil than that of the old knights—and he then received many potent arms, "Man-dart," "Fire-dart," "Man-eater"

"Ten-eyes," "Go where it likes," "Wounding at will"; and another ascetic Agastya gave him a bow and magic garments fresh from the hands of Viśvakarma, the Indian Vulcan. But one special weapon was given to the brothers, the famous Brahma-śiras, which had the wind for fathers, the god Agni for points, the Mountain Mandara in paradise for weight.

Here, again, we must call to mind that Hercules had the magical training of the early warrior. Castor, the son of Tyndarus, taught them how to fight; Eurytus how to shoot with a bow and arrow; Autolycus to drive a chariot; Linus to play on the lyre; Eumolpus to sing. The Centaur Chiron taught him battle-charms.

When the young Râma grew up he learnt that a peerless lady was to be the prize of a great competition at Mithilâ, a city in modern Tirhoot. She was the adopted daughter of King Janaka, and her name was Sîtâ, which means literally a "furrow." The gods of the Hindus had each a symbolical animal for his Śakti, or female energy. Śiva had a cow;

Brahmâ had Brahmî, "a swan." This gives the root meaning to the Greek story of Europa and the story of Helen, which both figure in the legends of Troy. Sîtâ was the name of the infant King Janaka, found in a furrow, and Sîtâ is also the name of Brahmî, Brahmâ's Śakti. King Janaka found a swan's egg, and Mr. Bryant[1] pointed out long ago that Helen was also thought to have been derived from a swan's egg, and that a fierce controversy raged about the spot where the egg was found, namely, ὑπερωον.

But here, by an Oriental scholar of importance, my manuscript has been assailed. It has been pointed out to me that I have confused the "Śakti" (literal "wife of the god") and the "Vahan," the heraldic animal representing him. Brahmâ's animal, I have been told further, was not a swan, but a goose. This criticism has proved of immense importance to me, but not in the direction suggested by my critic. I will consider the Śakti idea later on. A word about this goose.

[1] "Dissertation on the Trojan War," p. 11.

Linnæus ranks "goose" and "swan" under the word *anser*, which, pronounced by a Frenchman, would sound very much like the Indian word for "swan," *hansa*, pronounced nasally and without aspirate by a Hindu.

In the marsh land, which was much more plentiful than dry land in early days, the swan ruled. With his long neck and a power to keep his head under water, he ducked and suffocated rival birds that annoyed him. Colonel Moor, the eminent student of Indian mythology, opined that he was chosen as the Śakti of Brahmâ, because the swamp, with its land, indicated the earth, the manifested Kosmos, and with its water, the mysterious "waters" round the earth, the awful region where the unmanifested god was believed to dwell.

Then we know that the sooty petrel, the barnacle goose, and other geese that frequent swamps, have long necks, and are mistaken for swans.

But the selection of a swan for the Vahan of Brahmî has another explanation.

Says Byron: "Swans sing before they

die." Brahmî represents music in the form of a beautiful woman. Colonel Moor tells us that in her portraits she is always depicted holding a rude musical instrument, the Vîṇa, formed with two gourds. In Egypt also the swan as a hieroglyphic meant music, and in Greece the bird was sacred to Apollo and the Muses. Does not all this seem to point to an aquatic and musical *anser* rather than a barn-door *anser*, whose music is of doubtful excellence?

My critic formed his conclusions from a recent visit to the monuments of India. Colonel Moor, who studied these monuments for forty years, writes:

"Except in the Elephanta Cave, I do not recollect ever to have seen Brahmâ or his Śakti attended by the swan."

But it is fair to add that he in part confirms my critic. Modern Hindu art is not very happy in its studies of birds. Brahmî's swan is much more like a "paddy-bird (*bhagala*)," says Colonel Moor.

But here again we get a bird that frequents swamps.

One other point remains, because the whole of this is very important in our inquiry. If Brahmâ was not the Supreme God who parented Sîtâ, what other Supreme God could it have been? The only possible answer here is Indra. But Indranî's "Vahan" is an elephant. His offspring could scarcely have been concealed in a furrow.

But wherever she came from, Sîtâ was the sweetest character that it ever entered into the heart of man or god to conceive. Râma went to Mithilâ, and was introduced to the King, who told him that none could marry his daughter except the hero who could bend a mighty bow, the bow of Śiva.

It was suggested by Viśvâmitra, his *guru*, that his young pupil should try his prowess. The King immediately sent for the bow. It reposed in an iron case. Eight hundred athletes and eight wheels were required to bring it along.

"This," said the King to Râma, "is the Shining Bow. Many Kings have tried, but all have failed even to lift it. I have ordered

3

RÂMA WITH THE BOW OF ŚIVA (p. 70)

[Face

it hither, young Prince, according to your wish. Who can hope to string it and shoot with it!"

Buoyed up by the wise Viśvâmitra, the young sun-god opened the iron case. A breathless crowd looked on. Râma took up the bow and fixed a string to it. He adjusted an arrow, and, using all his force, he bent the mighty weapon. It snapped with a terrible uproar. The spectators fell to the ground stunned. It seemed as if the thunder-clap of Indra was reverberating amongst a thousand hills. The King was astonished.

"Venerable prophet," he said to Viśvâmitra, "I have heard of the brave young Râma; but what he has now done transcends mortal strength. I have promised my daughter Sîtâ as a prize to the strongest. With her let him raise up a mighty race, to be called the 'Sons of Janaka.'"

Swift messengers were sent to King Daśaratha to tell him of Râma's luck.

"King Daśaratha came to the wedding accompanied by his two younger sons. It was arranged that the marriage should be quadruple. A sister of Sîtâ was given to Lakshmaṇa, and two nieces of Janaka were betrothed to the other brothers.

"And now in the 'place of sacrifice,' in a leafy cathedral perhaps, with its twelve huge, unhewn columns, the four moon-faced, large-eyed brides came tinkling along with their leg-bangles, and mincing in their gait like the daughters of Zion who irritated the prophet Isaiah. Their clear brown skins contrast with their cloudy muslins. Their jewels, it is said, made them sparkle like dancing flames. The sons of King Daśaratha were also bravely decked. Brahmins muttered their incantations and chanted their hymns. The offerings smoked up in the clear air. Each Prince advanced and gave his hand to his bride. The four couples then marched round the flaming altar with measured steps. Three times this rite was repeated. A prodigy crowned the feast. Flowers not grown in earthly gardens were showered upon the young couples, and the soft strains of the Gandharvas gave the mortals present a taste of heavenly minstrelsy."

There is a calm here, and the author seems optimistic and petty; but he never loses sight of the fact that he has a very serious story to relate, and he strikes a deep note very early. The flatteries and bridal splendours of Mithilâ are as bubbles above very deep waters. It is a battle between good spirits and evil spirits. He invents names, he invents details, but it is a real battle which he believes to be going on under his eyes.

After the wedding, King Daśaratha starts to return to his capital accompanied by Vaśishtha, but it is recorded that "the birds, heralds of calamity, seemed all to fly to his left hand."

"Why, O teacher," said the monarch alarmed, "do I see this prodigy, and why is my pulse fluttered and quickened?"

The hermit Vaśishtha pointed out that the stags and hinds had skipped about to the right of the travellers.

But the monarch's pulse was destined to be more fluttered still.

Suddenly a strong wind arose which

whirled the dust into strange shapes and darkened the welkin.

The sun lost its heart, the universe was soon a mass of fine powder. The bodyguard of the King was beside themselves with fear.

This was another bad presage for the story of the poor bride Sîtâ, one of the most pathetic stories that ever was told.

But we must now return to King Daśaratha.

"Perhaps the worst evils of polygamy are the cruel rivalries of the palace. Each queen strives to get her son nominated heir to the royal umbrella. To effect this, the murder or mutilation of his rivals is considered quite lawful. And the interests even of the father are made quite secondary to those of the boy. When the English Government got into difficulties with Shere Ali of Afghanistan, it is no secret in diplomatic circles that one of his queens volunteered to murder him if the succession were secured by the English Government to her son. A zenana is of necessity a divided house, and a state ruled from the zenana a divided kingdom.

"The poet of Ramâyâṇa has based the

dramatic interest of his story on these truths. It was the misfortune of King Daśaratha that his favourite son was not the offspring of his favourite queen. This was the hidden calamity that made the birds of the air fly to the left, and the dust whirl in darkening circles about the skies.

"One of the brown-skinned, large-eyed queens of King Daśaratha was named Kaikeyî. She was beautiful and attractive, silly and jealous. This jealousy was fanned by a malicious female slave. She accosted her mistress one day. 'Awake, O foolish queen. See you not that you are lost? Râma is pronounced the heir of the King.' Outside, the city streets were noisy with preparations for the coming consecration.

"'What is the meaning of these words, Mantharâ?' said the queen, with much surprise.

"'You are nursing a serpent,' said the slave, 'and a serpent stings. See you not that the rise of Prince Râma means the disgrace and ruin of your son, Prince Bharata. The king has befooled you with sterile blandishments and empty dreams, and will now give you a prison for a portion!' With speeches like these the jealousy of pretty and silly Queen Kaikeyî was fanned. The slave pointed out also a substantial danger that exists in all Indian courts. When a young prince comes to the throne, he banishes or assassinates his younger brothers.

"Queen Kaikeyî was soon beside herself with rage and fear. 'What is to be done?' she said, with breathless excitement.

"'Do you not remember, O queen, a promise of the king? In ancient days, when he came back wounded from a war, you tended and cured him. His Majesty then pronounced these words, "Ask me a boon—two boons—and I will grant them!" That promise has not yet been fulfilled. Demand that Bharata shall be consecrated as heir to the throne, and Râma banished to a desolate forest!'

"The boldness of this proposal took the queen by surprise. But the persevering slave was not to be balked. She arranged a clever comedy for the ill-fated king.

"In the women's apartments of an ancient Indian palace was a Chamber of Pouting. If any queen grew out of temper or jealous, this chamber was always ready to receive her whilst the fit lasted. By the advice of the slave, Queen Kaikeyî prepared what modern husbands call a 'scene' in the palace of Ayodhyâ. King Daśaratha was summoned thither in hot haste, and what did he see? His favourite wife, the lovely Kaikeyî, lying on the bare ground, and weeping scalding tears. Her splendid tiara of pearls and diamonds was flung at her feet. Her glittering ankle-bangles and armlets were also scattered around. Silks were tossed hither and thither, and the rarest muslins. The pretty nails of the queen were no longer anointed with rare unguents of sandal-powder. The fine artistic touches of kohl that were wont to make her eyes sparkle like the eyes of a nymph of Indra, were now blurred with salt tears. The monarch, seeing the queen that he loved dearer than his life in this pitiable condition, sought to comfort her, as a noble beast when his consort in the forest is smitten with a poisoned arrow.

"'I know not, dear queen,' he said, 'the cause of this anger that you show me. Who has outraged you, that you lie thus in the dust on the ground? If there is an enemy to punish, a wrong to be righted, a poor man to be made rich, if you want more pearls, diamonds, emeralds, tell me, O woman of the heavenly smile. I am the king of kings. Name but your wish, and it is granted.'

"'No one has insulted me or vilified me,' said the queen, 'but in old days you made me two promises. Those promises I now wish to see fulfilled.'

"'They are granted,' replied the monarch. 'With the exception of Prince Râma, you are all that is dear to me in the world. Ask what you wish, and the boon is granted. I swear this on the integrity of all my past acts.'

"'When a king swears before Indra and

the heavenly hosts,' said the queen, 'before the Gandharvas and the spirits that watch over the homes of us all, we may be sure that he will keep his word. In lieu of Râma, consecrate my son Bharata, and banish Râma for fourteen years to the forests.'

"'Oh, infamous fancy!' said the king in his horror; and, torn between his love for Râma and his integrity, he fell senseless upon the cold ground. When he recovered, his remorseless wife was still at his side. He stormed at her, he railed, he entreated, he flung himself at her feet, and prayed her to withdraw her ungenerous demand. 'If for a moment I were deprived of the sight of my dear son Râma, my mind would not bear the shock. The world would be without its base, the grass without rain, my body without the breath of life!'

"'Once you were celebrated amongst just men as a man of truth, a man of integrity,' answered the queen. 'You promise, and now you refuse.'

"'The banishment of Râma, O ignoble woman, means my death.' And the painful reflection came into the king's mind that his memory would for ever be execrated as the dotard slave of a vain woman and the slaughterer of his son. And when, thought he, the holy masters call me to a solemn account, and say: Where is Râma? What shall I say?'

"'You speak as if I were the malefactor,' said the queen, with persistent cruelty. 'What fault have I done? The promise came from you, not me.'

"Thus, through a painful night, the poor king fretted in 'chains of fraud.' At times he flung himself at her feet, and tried senile blandishments and flatteries: 'Save a poor old man whose mind is getting unhinged. Sweet Kaikeyî of the gentle smile, take my life, my kingdom, my treasure, everything but Râma! Spare me! save me!'

"The poet records that once a king, having promised to save a fluttering dove that flew for protection to his bosom, engaged himself to give the pursuing hunter any other boon. 'Cut out your heart,' said the hunter. The king complied. Our poor, loving, senile old dotard has much now in common with that afflicted monarch.

"Morn came, but it brought no solace. The king's charioteer, who was poet-laureate as well as coachman, woke him up with a madrigal. Outside were courtiers and citizens in gala dress. They were collected to see the consecration of Râma.

"The king sent for his son.

"Forth drove the charioteer to the palace of the prince. Râma, summoned, started after exchanging a bridegroom's farewell with Sîtâ at the doorway. Strong demonstrations from the citizens greeted him in the streets. The populace idolized him. In his father's palace he found the king with Kaikeyî. The piteous condition of the former quite startled him. The poor old king could only just articulate the words, 'Oh, Râma!' and burst into a convulsion of sobs. Râma demanded of Kaikeyî the meaning of the king's grief. She told him bluntly the history of the promise and her choice—

"'My son Bharata is to be consecrated,

and you will be banished to the forests for fourteen years.'

"'If it makes my father any happier, I am ready to go,' said the prince simply.

"Soon the terrible news that the Prince was to be banished spread through the palace. Kauśalyâ heard it. The brothers heard it. All were in consternation. A trial greater than the long banishment was the task of breaking the painful intelligence to poor Sîtâ. Râma told her what had occurred. He exhorted her to bear his absence bravely, and comfort his mother. This was the answer of Princess Sîtâ—

"'Brave Prince, in mortal life
Men singly battle; good and evil deeds
Are theirs;
And each man reaps the harvest of his acts,
His own and not another's.
But woman clings to man,
For she is weak;
His lot is hers, and wheresoe'er he goes,
In briary paths or weary tanglements
She follows gladly.
By my great love I swear that reft of thee,
Protector, Master, Refuge, Patron Saint,

E'en Brahmâ's heaven, were dull.
Fathers and mothers eke,
Beloved sons and daughters, what are they?
A wedded spouse lives only in her lord.
Blind malice plots and wounds,
Laugh at her wiles, sweet Prince,
The shining towers of golden battlements,
Halls hung with silks galore,
Couches and odours sweet—
These, without thee, were as a desert waste.
In paths of banishment
I hang around thy feet—
Thy weary feet—dear spouse;
And the rude home of tiger, snake, and pard,
The thorns, the stony steep, the cataract
That bellows with the water of the storm,
And e'en the realms of anguish mortals feign,
As the grim goal of earthly infamies—
These by thy side were bliss.
Thou art my universe;
Thou art the form benign,
That speaks to me of heaven,
That speaks to me of love.
In wildernesses dank our holy men,
Clad in the bark of trees,
Dream holy dreams of God:
Thus will we live, and I will deck my spouse
With chaplets plundered in the hidden dells.'

"Râma remonstrates, and points out how little the silken days of her past life have fitted her for the terrible ordeal of the yogi in the forest. His other friends try to dissuade her. The spectacle of this old-world, brown-limbed, bold-hearted young woman, this high ideal of wifehood at the date of the poem, is quite extraordinary.

"A crowd of citizens accompany the poor exiles as they are driven by the faithful poet-charioteer out of Ayodhyâ. Râma is the idol of the populace. Lakshmaṇa has obtained leave to bear him company. The fond old king went out for a short distance with his son. He then watched him, departing in a cloud of dust. Râma's mother tried to comfort him in the palace. 'Râma is gone,' said the king. 'Some men are happy, for they will one day see him return. Not so his father. Touch me, Kausalyâ; I see you not.' The eyesight of the afflicted monarch had departed with his son."

Again we pause. If we nickname Daśaratha, Jupiter—and Kaikeyî, Juno, we get a startling string of coincidences. Can they all be perfectly accidental? A mighty war is raging between the powers of good and evil. Owing to some strange freak of the great Destiny which was believed in Greece, as elsewhere, to override even the gods, a mortal champion was wanted to secure the victory. Everything had been carefully planned out. Jupiter himself had gone down to Alcmena's bed to parent this unique hero. In the meantime all had been prepared as in India for the great battle. Mars the god of war, Neptune, Minerva, Athene, were ready for the struggle, and many enchanters, giants, and "hundred-handers." Then omniscient and all-wise Jove was tricked by a silly quibble. He had announced in heaven that the great hero would be born on a certain day. Juno, his wife, persuaded him to swear this on the water of the Styx—an inconceivable transaction when viewed on either side. Then by the aid of Lucina, the goddess, who presides at child-birth, Juno retarded the birth of Hercules, and produced a seven months' child Eurystheus, the son of Sthenelus, King of Argos, on the day on which Jove had promised the birth of a hero with absolute power. Juno interprets this to mean that the absolute power is placed in the hands of Eurystheus. Jupiter accedes to this gross absurdity.

Now let us put the two stories side by side:

1. In India the Champions of Right in their great struggle against the Cohorts of Evil are taught to rely on a mortal champion. A similar idea occurs in Greece.

2. The champion is born in India by the special supervision of Brahmâ and the gods. In Greece he has for sire the King of Heaven himself.

3. A light oath given to a pretty woman years before is brought up in India, an incomprehensible promise is fabricated in Greece.

4. The motive of the two women is the same. Râma must live for fourteen years amongst the wild beasts and fevers of an Indian jungle. Hercules must execute every dangerous enterprise that a hostile task-master can conceive for twelve years.

The death of each warrior is plainly sought.

This blindness seemed doubly calamitous to the old King, for he looked upon it as a visitation. Years before, when he was hunting in the forest, he approached in the gloaming a river where the deer and the buffaloes were accustomed to feed. Suddenly he heard a gurgling sound. Believing that some large animal was drinking, he let fly an arrow, and to his surprise heard a piercing shriek. He ran up and found a little boy writhing upon the ground. A broken water-jug was by his side.

"Oh, what merciless archer has done this?" cried the little fellow. "My father and my mother are both blind and helpless. I alone can fetch them water and food. Now they will starve. Why is this? What have I done that I should receive this cruel bolt? I had come to the river to get them water."

The face of the poor little boy was blurred with blood and tears. The King tried to comfort him, but he repeated:

"I alone can fetch them water and food.

Now they will starve. Now they will starve."

Soon the poor boy became insensible from loss of blood, and gave up the ghost. The King went round in search of the parents, and found them peevishly lamenting his long absence.

"Oh, where is our water? We are so thirsty. Where is our food?"

The King told them what had happened, and the old man was furious.

"Before you die, O Prince, you will lose your son in a forest, and you will become blind; mark my words."

A word here about Hercules and Dejanira. Like Râma, he conquered a beautiful wife at a Swayamvara by defeating all the other competitors. This was at the Court of King Æneus at Calydon. Then by a fateful accident he unwittingly slaughtered Eunomus with a blow of his fist. This preyed so on his mind that he and Dejanira fled from Calydon. Again we have strange similarities. Râma and Sîtâ are driven into the jungle through a fateful arrow, which accidentally causes death. Hercules and his wife are also exiled through a similar unwitting calamity.[1]

[1] This gives Baladeva, the Indian Hercules. He has in his hair the *balaband*, or "fillet," that Rajpoots to this day are proud of—the diadem of the Greeks. He has on his right arm the skin of a lion (*Bagambra*), and in his left hand a club, adjoining which is a "monogram of two letters of an ancient and undecipherable character found on monumental rocks and pillars wherever the Pandus colonized."

Colonel Tod considers all this—

1. To "confirm Arrian, who, two thousand years ago, drew a parallel between the costume and attributes of the Greek and Indian Hercules."

2. The strange monogram proves the antiquity of Indian gem-cutting, and the gem proves the antiquity of the Indian Hercules (*Journal Royal Asiatic Society*, vol. iii.).

CHAPTER V

STORY OF RÂMA CONTINUED

In the Forest.

THE first halt of the exiles was on the banks of the Tamasâ. Here was a thick wood, and Râma and Sîtâ slept under a tree on a litter of leaves. Each wore the apron of bark tied with a cord round the waist.

Râma escaped furtively next day from the banks of the Tamasâ, for the citizens still hung on his track. He made his way to the Gomatî (now the Goomtee), and by-and-by reached the Ganges at Śringavera, in the district of Allahabad. The poet-charioteer was here dismissed with a loving message to the old King. He was enjoined to be kind to Kaikeyî, and to forgive her. They then reached the hermitage of the holy saint Bharadwâja, at the junction of the Jumnâ and Ganges. At this very sacred spot is the modern Allahabad. By the advice of the sage they took up their quarters on the hill of Chitra Kûṭa, which is about two days' march from Allahabad, and situate on the River Piśunî. The holy hill of Chitra Kûṭa is now to the followers of Râma what the Lion Hill of Gâya is to Buddhists.

"How many centuries have passed," says Professor Monier Williams, "since the two brothers began their memorable journey, and yet every step of it is known and traversed annually by thousands of pilgrims! Strong, indeed, are the ties of religion when entwined with the legends of a country. Those who have followed the path of Râma from the Gogra to Ceylon stand out as marked men amongst their countrymen. It is this that gives the 'Râmâyaṇa' a strange interest; the story still lives, whereas no one now in any part of the world puts faith in the legends of Homer."[1]

"It is added that every cavern and rock round Chitra Kûṭa is connected with the

[1] Lillie, 'Buddhism in Christendom," p. 316.

names of the exiles. The heights swarm with monkeys. The edible wild fruits are called 'Sîtâ-phal.'[1] Vâlmîki, the author, lived here, and he has given his poems local colour.

"To cross the holy Yamunâ (or Jumnâ) a raft was made by the brothers of logs and bamboos. Sîtâ trembled at the sight of the gurgling current, and Râma held her in his strong embrace. Near the banks where they landed was a holy fig-tree (Syâma). 'Having adored that sacred tree, Sîtâ thus prayed to it with pious reverence: "May my stepfather live for a long time, lord of Kośala. May my husband live a long time, Bharata, and my other kinsmen. And may I see once more Kauśalyâ living!" With these words uttered near the tree, Sîtâ prayed to the holy fig-tree, which is never invoked in vain; and, having duly worshipped it by tripping round it from the right-hand side, the three exiles went on their way.'"[2]

I must mention here that there is a prominent distinction noticeable in the Indian epic

[1] "Indian Epic Poetry," p. 69.
[2] "Ayodhyâ Kandâ," cap. lv.

when we compare it with the Greek compositions. It is that in the "Râmâyaṇa" every god, every demon, every King, every soldier, every priest, and also every saint, is a student of magic. The details of the magical training of the Hindus are tolerably well known. To obtain superhuman powers a man must leave his ordinary business of life and become a Vânaprastha—a word that means an ascetic who retires to the solitude of the jungle to obtain visions and superhuman potencies. There he must sit patiently under a tree, like Buddha, "suppressing his breath," and going through other details of training for years, or, as the Indian books, with Indian exaggeration, put it, for hundreds of years. First there will come to him, he is told, visions of divine beings. And then he is promised other powers. He may make himself invisible; he may rise in the air; he may be able to swell out to an enormous size or to contract himself indefinitely; he may read thoughts and tell the future.

To understand the "Râmâyaṇa" all this must be kept in view. To ordinary English intelligence Vâlmîki must seem quite silly when he tells us that an omnipotent and supreme god like Indra could be overturned by another god, Śiva—or, worse, by a mere mortal like Râvaṇa—simply because the dethroning being had practised more "austerities," "treasures of mortification," etc.

And the rôle of Brahmâ in the epic must be equally incomprehensible. If his one object, and the chief object of the heavenly hosts, was to overthrow Râvaṇa, why did he give a spell to him, and pet Indrajit, and give him a title of honour? Plainly the Indians held that there was a vague something above the gods.

Ezekiel describes the women weeping for the god Tammuz. This is the lament of the women of Ayodhyâ for the god Râma. It has echoed in India for perhaps 3,000 years.

"THE LAMENT OF THE WOMEN."

"Weep, husbands weep,
For what are homes and wives and riches now
With Râma fled?
Afar the forests smile,
The brake with dainty flowers,
The lotus-covered mere,

The trees that climb the mountain, hiding fruits
    And honey, Râma's food.
Blessed rocks and thicket tangles ye that hold
    The gentle Lord of Worlds,
The Owner of the Mountains, and the Prop,
    The Champion of the Right.
    Days follow weary days,
    Each brings its guerdon sad;
Our sons grow up within our rayless homes
    Our homes bereft of hope,
    And full of woman's tears.
    Fraud reigns, the wicked Queen
    Yokes us like weary beasts;
    Soon the blind King will die.
    O Râma, come again!
    The shadow of his feet
Worship ye men, ye women bow your heads,
    To Sîtâ, blameless wife!"

"The fugitives slept that night on the banks of the river, and sped next morning through the forest.

"'See,' said Râma to his wife, 'the kinśuka with flowers that shine like flames of fire. See the pippula and the champaka. We have reached Chitra Kûṭa, and can live on fruits. The bees hum around and offer us their honey. Cuckoos sing to the peacocks. Here, O woman of the dainty waist, is joy for man and brute!'

"The brothers immediately set to work and constructed a rude hut for Sîtâ. It was made of supple boughs broken down by the wild elephants and covered with leaves. This rude hut, the pansil, is very prominent in Buddhism.

"When the hut was completed, Râma sent Lakshmaṇa to slaughter a stag with his bow. A rude altar was erected. Râma bathed to purify himself. The carcase of the stag was placed on the holy fire, and the proper incantations were recited. Offerings were then made to the dead ancestors. In this way the new domicile received the protection of the unseen intelligences. Portions of the deer were then eaten by the two brothers; and then the woman, Hindû fashion, contented herself with the broken victuals. Thus commenced their life in the green woods of Chitra Kûṭa. Round the rude huts the flowers clustered and the birds sang.

"Meanwhile the charioteer returned to the palace and announced that Râma had crossed the Ganges. The news was too much for the blind old king.

"'Touch me, queen,' he said to Râma's mother. 'Touch me, and I shall know you are there. If this hand were the hand of Râma, perhaps it would heal a malady that nothing else can cure. In fourteen years you will see him return with the mystic ear-rings. Like an old torch, my life is burning low!' That night he died, and his body was embalmed, to delay his cremation until Râma's return.

"On the death of the king, Bharata was summoned to reign in his place; but instead of being pleased with the machinations of his mother, he stormed and raved. He refused to accept the crown, and started off with an army of four corps—infantry, horse-men, chariots, and elephants — to bring Râma back. They stayed one night at the hermitage of Bharadvâja, and that great adept, by the power of his magic, was able to regale them all with flesh meat and wine.

"The necessity of a rigid observance of a promise, no matter what the consequences, is, perhaps, the noblest teaching of this fine old-world song. Râma, summoned to the throne, refuses proudly: 'Have I not pledged my word,' he answers, 'to the dead king, to remain fourteen years in the forest?'"

But now adventures begin to crowd. The brothers reach the celebrated Daṇḍaka forest, then spread all over Central India:

> "In that same wood of dire and awful fame
> Moved a foul fiend, Śûrpaṇakhâ by name;
> Foul Râvaṇ's sister, his domains she trod,
> And tricked the hermits from their dreams of God.
> Her bloodshot eyes possessed a tortuous stare—
> Much streaked her skin, and copper-hued her hair;
> In hideous folds her pendant cheeks did bag:
> A gross, incredible, ungainly hag.
> But she could change her shape by arts unmeet,
> And charm the hermits with love's counterfeit,
> Reducing for the nonce her monstrous waist,
> Pregnant with murder and with schemes unchaste.
> She and her brother Khara ruled the wood;
> Men were her meat, her drink was human blood."

Now Śûrpaṇakhâ "chanced to see the splendid figure of Râma in the green wood. His arms were long. His brow flashed with a heavenly shimmer. His eye beamed like the lotus. His limbs were the limbs of Kandarpa, the Indian cupid."

The feeling that she called her love was excited; and changing her form to that of a young and very beautiful woman, she accosted him:

"'Who art thou with the matted hair? . . . Thou bearest a bow and a quiver. Why hast thou sought these woods?'

"'I am Râma, the son of Daśaratha,' said the Prince.

"'I love thee,' said the demon. 'My power is immense. It can transport thee to distant steep, to hidden flowery dells. Fly with me, and taste joys unknown to mortals.'

"'I have a wife already,'" said Râma in great disdain." This speech turned Śûrpaṇakhâ at once into a bitter foe.

I said in my preliminary chapter that in my view the real forces battling in the "Râmâyaṇa" were the Aryan Brahmins opposed to Śivâ-Durgâ. This theory seems to be confirmed at every turn. What were the frightful wickednesses imputed to Râvaṇa and his crew? They interrupted the Brahmins in their sacrifices—that is, they were hostile to Brahminism. Also they were cannibals, eager for the hot blood of human victims. Now these failings are concentrated in Śûrpaṇakhâ, who is plainly the goddess Durgâ, without much disguise. She and her brother Râvaṇa are Śivâ-Durgâ. She is a cannibal, virulent against the Brahmins. Balked in her lust, she tells her brother Khara that she will eat up Sîtâ and Râma and Lakshmaṇa.

All this will be better understood if I give an extract from the ritual used in the worship of Kâlî. It is stated that a man offered to her will please her for a thousand years, and three men will insure her protection for one hundred thousand years. But the suppliant must speak thus :

"Hrang Hring, Kâlî, Kâlî! Oh, horrid-toothed goddess, eat, cut, destroy all the malignant. Cut with this axe; bind, bind; seize, seize; drink blood, spring, receive. Salutation to Kâlî."

By the side of this enticing witch, let us place the scene when Hercules met the young women at the parting of the ways. One, with rich attire and meretricious charms, offered him a life of luxury and earthly rapture. The second proposed a life of toil and self-respect. Hercules chose the nobler path; and the story is much used for its moral teaching, in the instruction of the young. But it seems to me to fit in very much better in the life of Râma. Did not Hercules seduce the fifty daughters of King Thespius?

Is the judgment of Paris a third version of this story? Durgâ, Śûrpaṇakhâ, and the Juno of the Achilles story, seem all the same person. The anger of contemned Juno causes the fall of Troy. The anger of contemned Śûrpaṇakhâ causes the fall of Laṅkâ.

Śûrpaṇakhâ, balked of her love, attacks Sîtâ, and Lakshmaṇa, in defending her, hacks off the demon's nose and ears. She brings up her brother Khara with an army to attack Râma, and he kills Khara and puts the army to flight.

An Indian surgeon, Dr. Hutchenson, has called attention to a curious point of analogy. Hesione, the sister of Priam, was carried away as a slave to Greece. Priam remonstrated and demanded her restoration. This being refused, he sent his son Paris, Hesione's nephew, to carry off a Greek lady, which was one of the chief forms of retaliation of those savage times. Here we have the nephew of Śûrpaṇakhâ attempting a retaliation also; one leading to the Siege of Lañkâ, and the other to the Siege of Troy.

Śûrpaṇakha hurries away to Lañkâ, and paints the charms of Sîtâ in warm colours:

"A wife Prince Râma owns,
With large round eyes and cheek divinely fair,
Pure as the moon her brow;
The locks that fall adown her neck
Outshine the clustering locks of Indra's nymphs;
Her waist is supple, and her shapely arms
Around a lover's neck
Were guerdon richer far
Than all the wealth that Indra can bestow;
Sîtâ her name. Away,
Away, and seize the prize—
Her beauty worthy thee.
Lakshmaṇ hath marred my face,
Our brothers in the earth,
Dâshaṇ and Khara, lie,
Their silent lips call mutely for revenge,
My wit shall aid thy strength,
A woman's wit,
And we will spoil Prince Râma."

This brings on the scene, the terrible Daśagrîva as Râvaṇ is called, the "Ten-headed." He is also called the "Demon who can change his form at will." Was not Helen first ravished by Proteus?

"Vast as the giant cloud that bears the storm,
He showed his dread, immeasurable form.
His arms were long, and copper-hued his eyes;
His wondrous heads seemed sheltered in the skies—
Each head a portent on the battle plain,
For cut it off, at once it grew again;
His mighty chest recorded many wars,
With wounds for chaplets and for trophies, scars:
This cut Kuvera made when wealth's proud lord
Was captured, he and all his mighty hoard;
And like the furrowing chasm on the plain,
When a great earthquake rips the world in twain,
Airavata's white elephantine prong,
(Indra's great elephant renowned in song)—
Made mark indelible to note the line it passed along.
The sun abashed invented a new road,
And passed dread Râvaṇ under his abode.
Foe to the Brahman Asrâms in the glade,
Their rites he sullied and their wives betrayed.
Giants his cohorts, cannibals his crew,
They fed upon the corpses that they slew.
And his great mouth—in realms of human pain
Is one such mouth, in Yama's dread domain—
A-hungered for all creatures that have breath,
Insatiate, immense, the mouth of Death."

Râvaṇa in his magical car Pushpaka speeds off to the Daṇḍaka wood, and has a conference with the demon Mârîcha. An infamous scheme is hatched. The demon, who has the power to change his form at will, assumes that of a beautiful antelope,[1] and comes close to the hut of Sîtâ. That lady, attracted by his seductive appearance, incites Râma and Lakshmaṇa to try and capture it without hurt. They pursue the gazelle; and soon a Brahmin mendicant appears at the door of the hut.

A covering of rough yellow shag was flung loosely over him. His matted hair was tied up in the orthodox Jâta. He carried an umbrella and sandals; and over his shoulders a dirty bundle. He had, moreover, a jug, and a staff surmounted with Sîvâ's trident.

He accosted the lady in bland terms, and she prepared to feed and entertain him as prescribed by the Śastras.

[1] An antelope! The most heart-rending story of India and the most heart-rending story of Greece are each ushered in with an antelope and an archer—Râma and his counterpart Agamemnon—and behind both are the Medusa features of Diana-Durgâ.

"It was the grim planet Śanaiśchara,"[1] says the narrative, "approaching the pale star Chitra."

The demon soon throws off his disguise and proposes to make her the head Queen at Laṅkâ, with five hundred waiting women and diamonds and pearls galore. Sîtâ is indignant, but helpless. The great demon seizes her in his arms and carries her off in the air.

A bird, Jaṭâyus, has been given by Râma to his wife as a companion and protector. It is more than a bird, a Deva in disguise.

This bird makes a tremendous effort to arrest the night-wanderer, as the sacred book always calls the evil spirits. He attacks Râvaṇa with talons and beak, but he is slaughtered and his carcase is burnt.

Sîtâ watches all this, and pours out a chant not without pathos :

"Who knows the signs ?
The language of the gods, a hidden lore,
Can tell what solid fortune dreams announce,
And note the false dream-stuff in palaces.

---

[1] Saturn or Śiva.

Thus it has been with thee,
O bird, my friend!
Great Râma, he of Raghu's race the pride,
Did give thee to his wife;
'Twas thine to stand by, watch her and protect her,
And thou art dead!
For her thou didst give up thy valued life
In battle proud.
Bird, thou wast more than bird!
At times I called thee Daśaratha, King;
At times I held that from the world of shades,
Bursting all doors his Sîtâ to be near,
In thy bright plumage Janak was concealed,
Janak, my sire!
Alas! that I should see
Thy plumes, that shone like Indra's gates of gold,
Gory and charred,
Thy wings all cinders.
Ah me! what wings will bear to Râma now
The tale of Sîtâ's capture by a fiend,
And tell him where to seek her?
And, sterner woe,
What wings will bear to him these tidings dire—
She met her death, but baffled the disgrace?"

Râvaṇa carries Sîtâ to Laṅkâ, which is a splendid city, decorated with the spoils that came to Râvaṇa through his victory over his brother Kuvera, the god of wealth. Columns of crystal and silver, and white marble and gold, support stately fanes and vast domes, gold bespattered. His palace "ravishes the soul," with "windows of ivory and gold, and tabernacles and pavilions. Splendid gardens surrounded it with amazing flowers." The fiend shows Sîtâ all this from a lofty pinnacle, and turns out diamonds and rubies by hundreds of thousands. He offers to make her his Queen; and threatens worse things.

Vâlmîki, in this very delicate situation, exhibits singular skill, and a high sense of what is pure and what is noble. Sîtâ's answers to the proposals of Râvaṇa are singularly dignified and brave.

"O giant King, give ear,
Free me and save thy soul!
Within thy breast a guilty hope abides
To hold me in thine arms
And seize a joy that ends in agony.
Thus in his fevered dream
The madman hopes to still
His pangs with poison.
Release the wife of Râma while you may,
Not long his vengeance stays,
Implacable as fate
It traverses the hills and seas and plains

That part the culprit and his punishment.
    Soon shall his twanging bow,
    His arrows flecked with gold,
    His dart of glistening steel,
    Grim as dread Yama's mace,
Disperse thine inky legions as the wind
Pursues the racing cloudlets white with fear.
    Legions on legions press,
    Their serried ranks shine out
    With gold and burnished brass,
They hurl defiance at my lion spouse:
    Thus it shall ever be.
His shining shafts through the complaining air
Shall speed to mar thy panoply and show.
In old wife lore the Indian fable runs
That dying men see phantom trees of gold,
    Look up, thy doom is near!
Not far the horrid regions red with lakes
Of human gore, the brake with thorns of steel
Prepared by Yama's justice for red hands,
    And breasts surcharged with lust.
    Thy threats and hopes are vain!
    My death an easy feat; a harder task
To shirk my Râma's unrelenting bolt."

We must now turn to the brothers, who, when they came back to their hut and found no Sîtâ, were quite beside themselves with grief and terror. Where could she be? What supreme disaster had occurred? They searched everywhere far and near.

They wandered about quite disconsolate, and had many adventures. Some of these seem to have suggested similar adventures in the "Odyssey."

The Cyclops.

The brothers came to a wood and Lakshmaṇa had at once strange forebodings of danger. These were promptly verified, for they beheld a prodigy—an enormous human trunk, the body of a giant. This body seemed to have no legs, nor could the young heroes detect any head attached to it, but in its chest there was a terrible eye—a solitary eye, enormous, wild, piercing—an eye that nothing could escape even at an enormous distance; and the monster had mighty arms, with which he seized bears, gazelles, tigers, elephants (all the large animals of the forest), and brought them to a gigantic mouth, which was also in his chest. This was a magician called Danu, who by his ascetic training had become so powerful that he could not be killed by gods or men. Of this he had boasted to Indra, and the God, to punish him, had made him swallow his own legs and head, and had then allowed him to live on, deformed, cursed, abhorred by all living creatures. This giant promptly seized the two Princes with his long arms, and tried to draw them to his large mouth. It was all they could do to stop him when he had got them as far as his huge lips.

"What spruce young warriors are these?" said the giant. "You carry bows and arrows, and you come to my forest, which folks call the Terrible Wood, as food for a hungry giant."

Râma, in his love agony, was ready to face death, but Lakshmaṇa was more matter-of-fact. "Let us draw our swords," he whispered, "and each hack away at an arm." This they did, and they promptly dismembered the big giant, and eventually killed him.[1]

But this adventure had an important sequence. The giant was so pleased to be at last freed from his fantastic and loathsome

[1] "Aranyakanda," vol. iii., cap. 64, ver. 14 *et seq.*

carçase by the brothers that he did them a good turn. His unseen spirit addressed them :

"O illustrious offspring of Raghu," said the voice, "thou seekest the peerless bride named Sîtâ. Speed off to Kishkindhyâ. There in a cave is the deposed King of the country, Sugrîva by name, with his minister, Hanuman. He can give thee tidings of her."

Monkeys and Bears.

We now come to chapters of our story that require a few preliminary remarks. The army of Râma which set out to rescue Sîtâ was composed of monkeys and bears. Modern Oxford professors can scarcely find language strong enough to deride these chapters. Professor Monier Williams is aghast at this "wild hyperbole," and Professor Max Müller thinks these poems—and, indeed, all other old Indian writings except the "Rig Veda"—pure nonsense, "wild and fanciful conceptions."[1]

[1] "Chips from a German Workshop," Max Müller, vol. ii., p. 75.

But side by side with this fact we must place another:

The "Râmâyaṇa" is by far the most successful work of fiction that the world has seen. It has been running some thirty, perhaps forty, centuries,[1] and is more popular now than at starting. Two hundred and fifty millions of Hindus still delight to listen to its verses.

The present writer, in the old days, when serving in India, has heard its verses chanted by a watch-fire after a day's march. Many sepoys could still sing most of it from memory. At the commencement of our march each day the sepoys all shouted: "Jy Râm! Râm!" ("Victory to Râma").

By the help of modern railroads, pilgrimages of proportions quite formidable, now take place annually to Chitra Kûṭa, near Allahabad, to the jungle where poor Sîtâ dropped her tears. They place all records of similar gatherings at Mecca, or the Holy

[1] The French Sanskritist, M. Fauche, dates it at 1320 B.C. Gorresio, the Italian translator, dates it 1400 B.C.

Sepulchre in Palestine, quite in the shade.[1] Now, Professor Monier Williams, having lived all his life in England, criticizes the poem as he would Malory's "Morte d'Arthur," a work dealing with ideas long since dead; whereas the early Orientalists, Colebrooke and Moor and Wilson and Tod, living amongst the Hindus, were able to see an India changed very little from the India of Vâlmîki. That poet was writing for the Hindus; he lived amongst the Hindus; he shared their creeds, aspirations, conventional fancies. Supernatural beings in India are still viewed as enormous giants. One has the head of a monkey, one has the head of an elephant, a third is a serpent. If this fact of the gigantic nature of the Indian gods is overlooked, the key to the "Râmâyaṇa" is lost. The bears are compared to huge dark clouds seen in the gloaming. The weapons of the monkeys are big rocks and tree-trunks.

[1] I read in a newspaper that these pilgrims now amount to 2,000,000 souls, all sects sending their share. An officer, whose regiment is at Allahabad, tells me that 1,500,000 is certainly reached.

8

The rock flung by Angada at Indrajit kills the four tigers and the charioteer of his car, and knocks down and stuns the giant, who is as tall as the Nelson monument in Trafalgar Square. In the Indian Battle of the Gods all are gods or demi-gods except Lakshmaṇa and Râma.

Says Professor Monier Williams: "Those who have followed the path of Râma from the Gogra to Ceylon, stand out as marked men among their countrymen. It is this that gives the "Râmâyaṇa" a strange interest; the story still lives: whereas no one now, in any part of the world, puts faith in the legends of Homer."[1]

And yet the Professor apologizes quite humbly when he presents to Oxford one or two very brief specimens of the poem. But if he had remembered at the moment that Homer, Milton, and the author of the Apocalypse have all pilfered freely from Vâlmîki, he might have judged that the great shock that he was about to give to the subacute literary fastidiousness of the Verdant Greens

[1] Monier Williams, "Indian Epic Poetry," p. 68, quoting *Calcutta Review*.

of the University was not likely, in the end, to do irreparable harm.

And now the most striking character appears upon the scene. You cannot call him the low comedy character of the piece; Vâlmîki intended nothing of the kind. But when, in a village, a rude dramatic version of Râma's story is given, and the most crafty and bustling agent of the piece at critical moments is a monkey, you can understand that village audiences would make him their favourite, and take him very much from his comic side.

Hanuman was at once monkey, giant, and the most potent of enchanters. He was the son of Pavana, the Wind. He could become as small as a mosquito or fifty times as big as an elephant at any moment.

This is his description: "His form is as vast as a mountain and as tall as a gigantic tower; his complexion is yellow, and glowing like molten gold. His face is as red as the brightest ruby, whilst his enormous tail spreads out to an interminable length. He stands on a lofty rock and roars like thunder.

He leaps into the air, and flies among the clouds with a rushing noise, whilst the ocean waves are roaring and splashing below."

He is the most popular of Indian gods, and, unfortunately, this description is a little too closely followed by the sculptor. He figures as yellow as gamboge, and his face is as red as a brick. Modern trippers in India ask: "What is that sugar-loaf in his hand?" It is the Himâlaya Mountains, which he brought down, with their herbs and simples, to cure Lakshmaṇa. Of that more by-and-by.

The brothers in due course of time found Sugrîva and Hanuman in their cave. Sugrîva had been deposed by Bâli, but when Râma tried to make an alliance with the King of the monkeys, Sugrîva was alarmed at the proposal.

"See those palm-trees, with long stems and cascades of graceful foliage high in the air. One day my brother Bâli sent an arrow through the stout stems of three of them."

"Illustrious King," said Râma, "complete

trust is important in war. You doubt my prowess. I will show you what I can do."

Now, there were seven palm-trees, all ranged in a line. Râma, taking up the bow of Śiva that he won when he competed with the suitors for the hand of Sîtâ, aimed an arrow at this line of stout trees. It passed through all seven, roaring like the thunder of Śiva, and flew to the regions of Yama; and by-and-by came gently back to Râma's quiver.

An alliance was formed between Râma and the Monkey King, and by Râma's directions four apes were sent off by Sugrîva to search for Laṅkâ. Their names were, Hanuman, Nîla, Angada and Jâmbavât.

But they could obtain no information as to the whereabouts of Râvaṇa; and Hanuman and Angada nearly lost their lives in a Golden Cavern.

Did this suggest the story of the sirens?

The Golden Cavern of the Five Apsaras.

Of old, says the Indian epic, there was a Vâna-prastha named Mâṇḍakarṇi who so mortified his flesh that by-and-by he got to threaten Indra's supremacy. For ten thousand years he had no bed nor seat but a rough stone, and no food but the wind. Indra was thoroughly alarmed at these abnormal austerities. He sent off five of his most beautiful Apsaras to tempt Mâṇḍakarṇi. They surrounded him with their celestial blandishments, and sang to him the songs of the heavenly choristers. Hanuman and Angada came to the spot where Mâṇḍakarṇi had lived. There, now, is a lovely lake called the "Lake of the Five Apsaras." Wild swans and the Sarali-thrush swim in its waters, and lotuses of many colours abound. And on a still evening soft voices can be heard from the depths, accompanied by delicious music. For below is a palace as enchanting as that of Undine. There

Màṇḍakarṇi is kept in sweet but efficient confinement by the Five Apsaras.

The pair foụnd their way through labyrinthine passages into these underground splendours, trees with gems and golden fruits. And then they found that they could not get out again. That was the usual fate of the rash adventurer. He left his bones in the cavern. This seems more logical than the Greek story. The sirens are gratuitous assassins. But the Apsaras, that tempt ascetics, had an object—namely, to prevent an ascetic magician from becoming too powerful. Svayamprabha on this occasion appeared and rescued them.

But help by-and-by came from a vulture named Sampâti, a brother of Jaṭâyus. He saw poor Sîtâ in the flying car; and she cried out, "Râma! Râma," as she went by.

He tells them that she has been carried to Laṅkâ; and that Râvaṇa lives at that place. To it he guides them.

By-and-by they reached the seashore and found that its terrible billows parted them from the spot they sought. How were they to get across? They were informed by Sampâti that a jump of 100 yoganas was necessary. What monkey or bear was ready to try either to jump, or swim, this distance? All declared that Hanuman, the son of Vayu (Indian Æolus), was alone fit to attempt it.

Hanuman, deputed to make the attempt, sprang into the water, and the waves for miles bubbled and raged against the rocks and coast with a mighty splash.

Now, it happened that between India and Lañkâ was a colossal submarine mountain. This mighty mass had been placed there by Indra to imprison the vast and potent demons confined in hell; the poet throws off all disguise at this point and confesses bluntly the real nature of Lañkâ.

The mountain was called Mainâka, and a sea-nymph dwelt among its grottos. She thus addressed it:

"The King of Gods, O Mainâka, hath placed thee here as a barrier before the cohorts of the Asuras who dwell in the lowest hell. Thy tall pinnacles remain here closing the gate of the boundless Pâtâla (hell) against the colossal Yakshas, who without thee would escape" ("Râmâyaṇa," vol. v., chap. vii.).

Then this sea-nymph, who has espoused Râma's side in the contest, orders the mountain to rise above the level of the sea to give Hanuman a resting-place half across the straits. This is done, and the various peaks that emerge, help eventually the army of Râma to build the bridge that carries them over.

When Hanuman was swimming, the demons incited a mighty nâga named Surasâ to stop him.

"Take," they said, "the shape of a fearful demon, vast as a mountain, with long and startling tusks, and yellow eyes, and jaws which when fully opened could touch heaven." The female Surasâ obeyed and confronted Hanuman with this:

"Come into my mouth," said the fiend to the monkey. "None can escape me that try to pass these waters."

"Your mouth is not big enough," said

Hanumân, and he suddenly made his body 30 yoganas long and 10 yoganas broad.

The female demon, undisturbed by this, made her mouth 10 yoganas across.

Hanuman then increased his form, and the female demon did the same, until at last it reached the enormous figure of 100 yoganas.

Then Hanuman contracted himself into a miniature monkey and ran down the demon's throat. Then becoming gigantic he burst the demon's belly. One version calls her Sinhikâ.

Here, again, we must turn to the life of Hercules. King Laomedon of Troy was obliged to place a young maiden, chosen by lot, on the shores of the sea every year to be eaten up by a sea-monster. On one occasion the lot fell on Hesione, the King's daughter. Hercules came to her rescue, and attacked the foul monster, jumping into his belly and slaughtering him as Hanuman slaughtered Surasâ. Again the old question confronts us:—which seems the most likely to have been the original story? The Indian narrative of an enchanter small as a mosquito when he ran down the demon's throat, and then growing as big as the Isle of Wight, or the Greek story of a human athlete forcing his way through the crunching jaws, say, of a megatherium.

And again strange evidence, roundabout, perhaps, but instructive, suggests itself.

What was the early Greek idea of hell? It is given by Hesiod: "A broken anvil," he says, "flung out from heaven would continue falling day and night for nine days before it reached the earth; and thrown out from the earth would take the same time to reach hell." Homer makes Ulysses visit hell; but does he tell the same story? Ulysses steered to the Cimmerian land with his followers; and they moored their ship. Sacrifices and solemn rites were paid to "all the phantom nations of the dead"; and the infernal halls were entered. Minos presided with his judgments and punishments. Sisyphus rolled his stone. Tantalus snatched at phantom grapes and figs. Plainly it was the conventional Greek hell, and on the seashore like Laṅkâ.

CHAPTER VI

RÂMA'S BRIDGE

THE army had now reached Adam's Bridge. How was it to get across? The work of the poet is to objectivize dreams—dreams of an individual—dreams of a nation. Vâlmîki found here singular assistance. Huge boulders, moved about by ice-action, are sprinkled along from the Himâlayas to Adam's Bridge. Then the Island of Ceylon, which was once a part of the Continent, has a reefy barrier which looks like a broken pier. This now goes by the name of Râma Setu (Râma's Pier). Two islands—one the Râmesurum, or Pillar of Râma, in line with the reef, keep up the fancy. Râma's island is crowned with a Cyclopean temple.[1] The

[1] The Râmeśwar, the goal of 1,000 pilgrimages, is one of twelve great Lingams, set up, it is said, by Râma

THE CHOULTRY AT RÂMÉSURAM

(PILLAR OF RÂMA)

[Face p. 124

broken line of the Setu, or pier, is sufficiently continuous to force all ships to pass round Ceylon altogether when sailing to or from the Ganges. When we add that the hill of Govardhana, near Muttra, and the whole Kymar range in Central India, also fit in to the suggestion that the Setu was created by huge Cyclopean giants, bringing, and also dropping, boulders and mountains from the Himâlayas to Adam's Bridge, the reader will think that Vâlmîki was happily helped by geography. His story tells us that at this point the giant monkeys went off to the Himâlayas, and brought boulders, small hills and large hills; and all worked to set up Râma Setu (Râma's Pier), which was at last happily finished. The fifth book that tells all this is called the Sundara Kâṇḍa, "the beautiful book," by the Hindus. This enrages Professor Monier Williams more than anything else in the "chain of absurdities" written by the poet Vâlmîki.

---

on the intervening island. Why Lingams? The spots had plainly an earlier, or Śivan, sacredness.

I don't quite know what to say to this. If I were told that a man named Brown and another named Harris lifted up between them a locomotive on the Great Western Railway on the 3rd of last June, and carried it 30 yards, I should say that the story was extravagant ; but when I have to deal with a power not of the earth, an almighty agent, I have to confess that the problem is beyond me. Professors of Oxford, happily gifted with a penetration which allows them to settle how much miracle may be allowed to a God Almighty, are, of course, under a different law. The monkeys were divine beings. On the surface Vâlmîki had a delicate task. He had to objectivize the religious thoughts and popular dreams of India. Aided by geology and geography, his work, on the surface, seems to have been signally successful. Perhaps the legend of Cyclopean builders, and dropping rocks, was in the Hindu mind before he touched the story. On it he has founded a poem that has moved and delighted more men and women than, I had almost written, all the other poems in the world put together. Two millions of Sîtâ's lovers go every year in pilgrimage to the spot where she garlanded wild flowers on Râma's brow.

Pâtâla, the hell of the Hindus, if Laṅkâ be a correct picture of it, is certainly not at all bad. The Queen-Mother Nikashâ, the favourite Queen, Mandodarî, and the brother of Râvaṇa, the giant Vibhîshana, all disapproved of the treatment of Sîtâ, and strongly urged Daśagrîva to return her to her husband. Vibhîshana, as I have already mentioned, plays the rôle of Antenor in the great drama. By-and-by Râvaṇa will insult him beyond endurance, and he will go over to Râma's army, and give it considerable help.

Meanwhile the poor Queen Sîtâ was in pitiable straits. She was terribly treated by the Râkshasas of Râvaṇa, the female friends to whom she had been consigned by Daśagṛîva. These fiendesses had strange names: "Ajamukhî" (Goat-head), "Haya mukhî" (Horse-head), "Lean-hips," etc. They threatened to kill and eat her; and certainly would have killed her with fright, if the Prophetess Trijaṭâ had not appeared on the scene. This caused the female goblins to run towards the witch to hear the news. They were goblins, but they were also females. Sîtâ took refuge in despair by the trunk of a Sinsapa-tree; and a little bird came and settled on a branch near her, and piped a little song, which seemed to say: "Be of good cheer, O daughter of Janaka. Aid is coming."

And now another strange incident occurred; a small monkey was hopping from branch to branch, and these words came to the afflicted Princess:

"Queen, nourished in the Videha, thy husband, the brave Râma, sends thee a message."

Sîtâ could scarcely believe her eyes or her ears. She saw the little monkey, and said in her soul: "Is it all a dream?"

"Answer me this," pursued the voice. "I seek Queen Sîtâ. A minute or two ago I saw a beautiful Queen blazing with jewels. She was seated by the side of a King, and many courtiers surrounded them. The pavilion where they reclined was all precious stones and sandal-wood. I said in my heart Sîtâ, the wife of Râma, could never sit thus beside another man. And now I see a woman in the ashes and rude garb of a holy ascetic. Tell me the truth, art thou Sîta?"

"My name is Sîtâ," said the lady, "and I am married to Râma the King."

"I come as his messenger, and I have passed the sea. His vast army is following—hundreds of thousands of bold warriors. They tramp along like the hosts of Indra when assailing the Maruts. Behold this ring which I have brought thee. See, it is inscribed with Râma's name!"

Sîtâ took the ring with immense joy. At first she had suspected some treachery.

"And now, Queen, come with me; I will carry thee safely to thy husband."

The Queen was astounded at this, the monkey was so small.

"I guess thy puzzle," said the monkey, "but see, I am now a giant. With these arms I will bear thee; and I will trample on all the soldiers of the Ten-headed."

By this time the monkey had shown his vast proportions..

The Queen replied with spirit:

"At the altar of Heaven, O gracious Vanar, I made a solemn vow that no arm should ever encircle me save that of Râma the King. That vow binds me until my death, be it far or near."

And no persuasion of Hanuman could shake this resolution.

But the persecutions of Râvaṇa and his furies by-and-by become more than human nature could bear. She determines to starve herself to death. But Indra visits her, accompanied by the god of sleep, whom he orders to throw into a profound slumber the hags and fiends that watch over Sîtâ. Then a grave and solemn old man appears before her, and addresses her:

"'Daughter of Mithilâ's anointed King,
Look up and listen to the news I bring;
To rescue thee thy spouse is on the way,
His dense battalions marshalled for the fray,

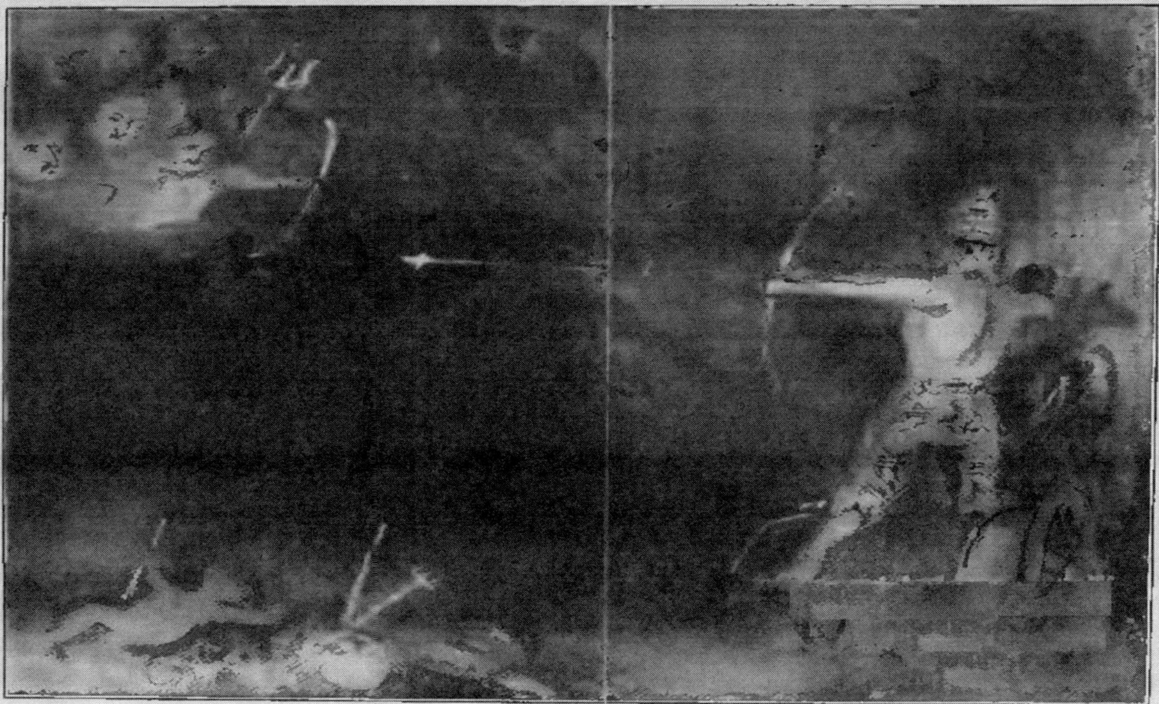

"AMAZING LEGIONS MUSTERED IN THE SKIES"

Face p. 120

Vanars with tree trunks, Devas in disguise,
Amazing legions mustered in the skies;
Not Râvaṇ's serpent-shafts, not boiling sea,
Shall keep thy Râma long from him and thee:
But list, brave spouse, to what the heavens have taught,
To starve is sinful whatsoe'er the thought;
The fates allot to mortals at their birth
A fixed amount of joys and woes on earth.
On rude sky pathways woes are help divine,
Great child of Janak, few to equal thine,
Thy guards through me are helpless in a swoon,
Drink of this milk—not paltry is the boon,
The nourishment of gods, the famed Amṛit—
For thy large sorrow some reward is meet.'
She answered, 'Man of aspect grave and just,
Whom in this realm can tortured woman trust?
Thy words bring hope to unexampled ruth,
Declare, O Ṛishi, swear thy words are truth.'
Up from the ground the stranger seemed to rise,
And showed confessed the Monarch of the Skies;
She drank the Ichor, and, like helpful balm
Mixed with huge terror, came a holy calm."

Monsieur Fauche has pointed out that, in Book XIX. of the "Iliad," Achilles in his great grief for the death of Patroclus has determined, like Sîtâ, to refuse all nourishment. Jove sends Minerva to give him the ambrosia of the Greek gods—which is the Amṛit of India.

"He spoke; and sudden, at the word of Jove,
Shot the descending goddess from above.
* * * * * *
To great Achilles she her flight address'd,
And pour'd divine ambrosia in his breast,
With nectar sweet, (refection of the gods!),
Then, swift ascending, sought the bright abodes."

This suggests a question. Who would be the most likely to earn an unexampled instance like this of divine sympathy, a boisterous swashbuckler with a bevy of "captive virgins" in his tents, or a noble woman in the toils of a lustful fiend? Another question. Why did Jove miraculously reinvigorate his most formidable opponent in the revolt of the gods?

And in the Court of Laṅkâ was an Indian Cassandra who spoke words of doom. Her name was Trijaṭâ. This was her vision:

The great city of Laṅkâ was throwing up flames and smoke to the skies. The hungry sea was toppling down spires, arcades, palaces. Vast hordes in red flickered before her eyes. They were bald-headed, drunken and dancing, and singing to the sounds of trumpets and tom-toms. Fearful words were heard at intervals. "Fly! fly! kill! kill!" Wild asses, an awful portent, were hurrying heroes to a lake of mud.

Then Râma appears in an ivory car, which is dragging a human being. Positively it is Râvaṇa, "with a cord round his neck being pulled towards the regions of Yama."

Here again is a very strange coincidence. Mr. Gilbert Murray has pointed out that in the Greek tragedies Hector was alive when first fastened to the car of Achilles. Râvaṇa is also alive, because he has not yet reached the regions of Yama, that is Death.

Râma's army by-and-by reached the sea. A bridge was built on the straits by the monkeys. Soon a fierce battle took place.

> "Now man to man selected foes engage,
> Or cohorts shock and crumble in their rage;
> Fierce arrow flights the demons pour like rain,
> And in their chariots race along the plain;
> Huge elephants like rounded clouds at dusk
> Trample on hosts, and ply the bloody tusk;
> Turmoil and scramble follow their attacks,
> Not men but cohorts fight upon their backs.
> The monkey army bravely bears the shock,
> Wields the great tree and aims the flying rock;
> The giant bears, disdaining distant strife,

Close with the demons and squeeze out their life.
Their coal-black forms show huge in clouds of dust,
Sharp claws and teeth the weapons that they trust.
Brave Jambumâlî fighting in the van
Pierced with his lance the breast of Hanuman.
The mighty giant crushed him with his fist,
And sent his soul to Yama's realms of mist.
Then Vibhîshaṇa, shocked at Râvaṇ's rape,
In Râma's battle ranked his awful shape ;
Him from his car with shafts Mitraghna plied,
But one huge javelin stopped his airy ride.
Great Virûpâksha braves proud Lakshmaṇ's might,
And Râma meets four champions in the fight.
The noise of battle spreads from shore to shore,
And bears and tigers drown the ocean roar.
Horses and monkeys grieve in woeful tones,
And all the breeze is charged with human groans ;
Ear-splitting drums sound out and trumpets blow—
Loud jeers and battle screams from foe to foe,
And far-off jackals sound their piteous note of woe.
But who is this that from his whirling car
Sustains the legions and directs the war ?
Four angry tigers hurry him along,
Him and his golden car with diamonds strung ;
A pennon streams behind, and all behold
A glistening serpent stitched in strings of gold.
His name was Meghanâda, till that day
When Brahmâ crowned his prowess in the fray,
When awful Indra fled before his might,
And all the gods were worsted in the fight.
Said Brahmâ, then, as record of the feat :
'He conquered Indra, name him Indrajit.'

Now when his father Râvaṇ saw the brood,
Sugrîva's army from the Aśoka wood,
He sent young Aksha first to stem the tide,
Aksha his youngest offspring and his pride—
But Hanuman, inspired with giant ruth,
Dispersed the myrmidons and killed the youth.
Fierce Râvaṇ, then, astonished and dismayed,
At once called Meghanâda to his aid.
'Go forth my son,' he cried, 'and face to face
Confront and kill this Pride of Raghu's race!'
Then Indra's Victor proudly led the swarms
To counter-strokes and rallying feats of arms;
Full on the bears their fiery weapons play,
And monkeys fall in swathes like fields of hay;
Torn shields and corselets figure far and near—
The broken falchion and the twisted spear,
Huge swarms of arrows buried to the head,
And wheels of cars whose swift career is sped:
Giants and elephants bestud the plain,
Vast blood-soaked forms that ne'er will stir again.
Amazing night! It really seemed that none,
Monkey or fiend, would see the morrow's sun!
Amazing night! Of such the Śastras tell—
The Kâlarâtri—Festival of Hell.
Amazing night! Predicted to efface
Man's joys and pangs—to end the human race.

* * * * * *

But in the clamour whence this sudden hush?
Two mighty giants on each other rush;
One—Indrajit, who hopes the day to crown
With one o'erwhelming champion of renown;
And Bâli's son, inheriting the fire,

The mighty glow and cunning of the sire.
Where arrows rain intrepid Angad stands,
A rock—a mountain—in his awful hands;
Aloft it rises with a hurtling sound,
And in the air it circles round and round;
The curve complete, down comes the monstrous rock,
All earth and heaven's concave know the shock.
Tigers and driver perish in the fall,
And one amazing ruin covers all.
Loud shouts of triumph come from Angad's crew;
Blinded and dazed, the demon chief they view.
Angad runs on to kill the fiend outright,
When lo! the vision mixes with the night."

Indrajit, according to Monsieur Fauche, is the model that has suggested Hector to Homer. Certainly there are plenty of those coincidences which Professors Monier Williams and Jacobi think of such small importance.

1. Priam and Râvaṇa have each a beloved son conspicuous for his daring. Each is the champion of his army.

2. This son heads a mighty rally on the part of the defenders which very nearly overthrows the invading army altogether.

3. Each is overcome and to save his life he suddenly disappears by miraculous means.

4. Each has a magical weapon. The darts of Indrajit become active serpents; the lance of Hector smites a foe and then returns to the hand.

> "Then parts the lance: but Pallas' heavenly breath
> Far from Achilles wafts the winged death:
> The bidden dart again to Hector flies,
> And at the feet of its great master lies."
>
> POPE'S "Iliad," XX.

The magical shafts of Indrajit were "serpents in the guise of darts."[1]

The car of Indrajit goes of its own accord wherever he wishes it.[2]

It may be mentioned here that Râvaṇa, the father, had a dart like Hector's that returned to his hand after killing a foe.

But we must now show how Indrajit got his weapons:

> "Concealed in Laṅkâ, in a darksome wood,
> Was a round space, and there an altar stood:
> Thither that evening, balked in his emprise,
> Went Indrajit for hell's own sacrifice.
> His warlocks bring him flowers and bloody garbs,

---

[1] "Râmâyaṇa," VI., c. 20, ver. 9.

[2] *Ibid.*, c. 64, ver. 12.

Red turbans, woods, and shafts with cruel barbs
And other bloody arms to make a hedge
From baleful goblins in their sortilege;
Into this ring a black he-goat they urge
And lead the victim to the Thaumaturge.
His throat is pierced, they catch the spirting blood,
And ghee[1] is mingled with the purple flood.
Then, with a spoon containing double scoops,
Mage Indrajit for this rich ichor stoops.
The altar he anoints; and in the dark
Come flames ignited by no earthly spark.
These ardent prodigies combine their spires
And show the God of Subterranean fires.
The horrent spectre turns towards the South
And laps th' oblation with his fiery mouth;
From this each quaking necromancer draws
Prognostics, favouring proud Lankâ's cause:
Then from the potent blaze comes forth a car,
Horses superb, a miracle in war.
At will this chariot vanished from the sight,
Raced fast or slow, or turned to left or right.
On it are magic weapons, that send out
Serpents intelligent, that race about,
Pursue the flying foeman, and enlace
His throat in irresistible embrace."

Meanwhile Râma and his brother were fighting bravely. Lakshmaṇa had for antagonist Virûpâksha. Râma was assailed

[1] Clarified butter.

by Agniketu, Raśmiketu, Suptaghna, and Vajraketu. Lakshmaṇa conquered his opponent; and Râma sent his four assailants to Yama's domain. His awful missiles cut off all their heads.

But whilst they were fighting thus boldly, Indrajit, in his invisible chariot, suddenly assailed them. They sent arrows everywhere into the darkness. But the fight was unequal. Indrajit was able to hit them wherever he pleased, but he himself remained perfectly secure. At last the demon, finding that ordinary arms could not kill the brothers, had recourse to a terrible enchanted weapon. It sent a fearful serpent, which enlaced them, and tied the two brothers together, apparently deprived of life.

The effect of this catastrophe was immense. Sugrîva, Nîla, Hanuman, and the other chiefs came together. Copious tears were shed by the rudest animals of the army. The sight of the two illustrious sons of Daśaratha, still pale and bathed in blood, was heartrending.

The boastful Indrajit drove straight to Laṅkâ. He reported at once to his father:

"Thy foes, O son of Uśrava, are now no more!"

Râvaṇa was overjoyed. He thought at once: "When Sîtâ hears this she will join my zenana, and I will give her thousands of pearls and diamonds."

It then struck the malicious old goblin that the sight of the corpses of the two brothers would help his suit. He ordered his car to be harnessed, and made the female demons carry Sîtâ on it to view the dead bodies.

SÎTÂ'S LAMENT.

"They vowed they could read veiled heaven's designs,
The Holy Priests that looked me through:—
'Fine arms, fine figure,' the twelve great signs;
'Bright eyes and a face that 'twas bliss to view';
'A widow she
Will never be:
Her throne will stretch from sea to sea.'

"But where is my spouse, and where my throne,
O false expounders of coming years?
Time's mighty wave lays all things prone,
Bold Râma in blood, and me in tears.
What gods did deem
A mighty scheme,
Has mixed with the mists of an idle dream.

"The brothers had clothes that the devas lend
To ward off arrows by potent spell,
Weird weapons as well whose shaft could send
A thousand foes to the gates of hell.
But they suffered harms,
For demon arms
Can mock invulnerable charms.

"A peerless husband and love's content
Were bridal gifts to a blissful wife;
But poison was changed for blandishment,
And Râvaṇ he came to mar my life.
His mighty spell
Binds fast in hell
The woman whose sin is to love too well.

"The ken of the priest is stayed by a shroud,
And the ken of gods both small and great;
Daivan[1] he dwells behind a cloud,
A screen that none can penetrate.
One thing is clear—
With Râma here
I call aloud, and he cannot hear."

The poor Queen at this point burst into a flood of tears.

But a Râkshasî, a female demon who had been sent in the chariot to look after the Queen, tried to comfort her; this woman was Trijaṭî. She had become attached to the gentle Sîtâ.

[1] The Indian Destiny.

"Monarch," she said, "wherefore these tears?"

"Is not my husband killed?" said the poor Queen. "The illustrious descendant of Raghu lies transfixed with arrows."

"Go to," said the night wanderer, "an army that loses its chief flies like wolves and dogs. Observe the army of your husband. They are full of wrath, and cry aloud for the battle."

"We have had enough of battles, O Trijaṭî," said Sîtâ.

"And mark this, great Princess: Death discolours the face and mars the limbs. The hero that to-day shines like Kâma, the god of love, or Kartekeya, the god of war, becomes, on the morrow, swollen, discoloured, loathsome. Watch thy husband, O woman of Mithilâ; watch thy brother, the renowned Lakshmaṇa. They lie still, but their faces are not discoloured. They show not the change of death."

The woman Trijaṭî prophesied truly in the case of Râma. The loyal Vibhîshaṇa came up, and was able with his magical knowledge by-and-by to restore Râma to consciousness. When the Prince was able to take in what had occurred, and saw the body of his brother, he was terribly afflicted :

RÂMA'S LAMENT.

" With Laṅkâ's gloomy shore,
Say what have I to do, O cruel Fate ;
Thy false prognostics, bound around his head
In blood, dead Lakhsmâṇ lies.

" With Sîtâ, too,
Say what have I to do—a sterner thought ;
A wife as fair t'were easy to obtain,
But comrade, counsellor, and brother tried,
Prop to the weak, and calm to the despairing,
In what direction shall my footsteps turn
To find his like ?

" Two mothers claim my love ;
Kauśalyâ gave me birth and tended me ;
And Sumitrâ was married to my father,
And when I tell her that her son is dead,
Like the sea-eagle o'er the bellowing wave,
Her scream will pass, and she will say to me,
' Give me my son !' How shall I find him for her ?

" His mighty spear and shafts
Tore through the battle of the demon crew
And spread around dismay unquenchable—
And, like the sun who quits the world on clouds,
We saw his glory brightest at the end.

"A shame has come to me,
A mighty shame, a grief unbearable,
That I should e'er have brought him to this doom;
He raised my courage when it needed help,
Not now can he console.

"A comrade bold and tried,
He followed me to wastes calamitous,
And in return 'tis right I follow him
To the black palaces of gruesome Yama,
The King of Death.[1]

"Sugrîva, noble chief,
I promised victory, I promised spoils,
And Râvaṇ's throne to Vibhîshana bold,
Boasts empty all;
Lead forth the army back across the straits,
Let Angad guide the van with watchful care
Depart whilst yet you may.[2]

"Nobly you all have fought—
Angad, Mainda, Dwivida, Susheṇ;
Nor let us e'er forget
Sampâti and Śarabha and Gavûksha,
And many other chieftains silent now,
They fell like heroes.

---

[1] "Yet, my Patroclus! yet a space I stay,
Then swift pursue thee on the darksome way."
POPE'S "Iliad," XVIII.

[2] "Why leave we not the fatal Trojan shore,
And measure back the seas we cross'd before?
The plague destroying whom the sword would spare,
'Tis time to save the few remains of war."
POPE'S "Iliad," I.

"For man to cope with Daivan fell,
The mighty destiny that hides his face [1]
Is vain, Sugrîva.
And e'en should Victory smile,
With Lakshmaṇ's shameful death and Sîtâ's doom,
What happiness for me!"

This is a tremendous climax. Its pathos is scarcely outranged in the whole of the world's fiction. What a picture! What a background! And what a situation, worked up as it has been, step by step, from a long way off! Can the same be said of Homer's verses, when Achilles laments the fate of Patroclus? Let us compare the two. Lakshmaṇa from the day of his birth has followed Râma like a faithful dog. Of his own choice he went with him to a banishment in the pitiless forest that meant his own effacement. Willingly he accompanied his brother to storm hell, and slaughter the Prince of the devils—Vâlmîki paints with

[1] "The stroke of fate the strongest cannot shun:
The great Alcides, Jove's unequall'd son,
To Juno's hate at length resign'd his breath,
So shall Achilles fall! stretch'd pale and dead."
POPE: "Iliad," XVIII.

big brushes. Râma has a wondrous dower. He is promised the sceptre of India. He is promised an unexampled career. He is to be a man-at-arms unequalled in the world's history. He is to win battles that the gods themselves have despaired of. To him and his brother have been given enchanted weapons that nothing can resist; enchanted armour that nothing can pierce. Moreover, the young Prince has been given for a wife a lady whose sweet qualities and also whose beauty were pronounced peerless in her day; and they have set India raving about her for fifty centuries.

And now all these promises appear to the poor Prince to have been broken one by one. The sceptre of India comes to him, but a vow has been extracted that he will remain in the deadly forests of India for fourteen years, which practically seems to mean his extinction and the withdrawal of the boon. He is given a large army to battle with the Yakshas, but instead of victory comes humiliating defeat. He is given a pure and loving wife, but she has been captured by a fiend. And now comes the last blow of all. The charms and the invulnerable garments have proved a ghastly delusion as well as everything else. "Wind-dart," "Fire-dart," "Man-dart," have all failed, and nothing has come of "Bull," or "Man-eater," or "Ten-eyes," excepting this —that the corpse of faithful Lakshmaṇa lies buried in honourable gore, and poor Râma himself, smarting with many wounds, lies the next thing to dead beside him.

We now come to Achilles. Patroclus is called a "squire," but the chief military duty of these squires—namely, the driving of the chief's chariot—was performed by Automedon, a special charioteer, who alone could guide the deathless horses of Jove. Patroclus performed offices almost servile—roasting fat chines, pouring out wine to the guests, making up the bed of Phœnix, escorting slave-girls for other men. Also he considers Achilles a severe master. He says to Nestor:

"Well dost thou know, old man, fosterling of Zeus, how terrible a man he is; lightly would he blame even one that is blameless."

Now, it can scarcely be contended that the story of Achilles reaches the depths of pathos and the altitudes of religious feeling of the Indian story, nor can it be contended that that haphazard tale can vie with it in the matter of construction. Its crux is the affection of Achilles for Patroclus. But was he so very affectionate?

Says Achilles:

> "A generous friendship no cold medium knows,
> Burns with one love, with one resentment glows;
> One should our interests and our passions be;
> My friend must hate the man that injures me.
> Do this, my Phœnix, 'tis a generous part;
> And share my realms, my honours, and my heart." [1]

That is a fine passage, but it is not addressed to Patroclus, although it was uttered within a few hours of his death. And if we rise from mere technique to *motif*, can the thought that created Achilles and his petty squabble be compared for a moment to the thought that conceived Râma, his giant ambitions and his mighty woes? Achilles believed that he could give the victory to the beaten Greeks at any moment.

[1] Pope: "Iliad," IX.

"The glorious combat is no more my care;
Not till, amidst yon sinking navy slain,
The blood of Greeks shall dye the sable main;
Not till the flames, by Hector's fury thrown,
Consume your vessels, and approach my own:
Just there, the impetuous homicide shall stand,
There cease his battle, and there feel our hand."[1]

If he thought this, why did he send Patroclus, who had not been held by the heel in the Styx, to certain and unnecessary death? It may be urged that Patroclus was not intended really to fight; but a single warrior cannot put to flight an army of 50,000 men without some simulacrum of battle. Homer's borrowings seem haphazard and contradictory. Jove has one object, the safety of Troy, and yet we see him restoring with his ambrosia the ailing champion of the foe, and giving him his own chariot wherewith to gallop over the bold fighting-men that were loyally fighting his (the Thunderer's) battle. We see the god of the Greeks fighting against the Greeks; we see the champion of justice and purity defending rape and treachery and the breach of marriage vows; we see a fond father, the wielder of the terrible thunderbolt and the

[1] Pope: "Iliad," IX.

bearer of the ægis, unable to save his favourite son from a dressed-up mountebank, the mere simulacrum of a fighting-man; we see the omniscient hoodwinked by a pert young goddess, who is able to trick him out of his champion defender, the mighty Hector, by dressing up and personating that champion's arms-bearer, and then treacherously leaving him without arms in the middle of the fight; and, finally, we see the gods crowd eagerly round, not to watch a mighty struggle, as in India, where wrong is pitted against right, and the false and malignant gods of a vast tract of country are battling for supremacy with the pure gods of another huge region, but to behold the caprice and braggadocio exhibitions of Achilles. In an earlier Greek myth, Castor and Polydeuces and Helen are all three children of Jupiter. The Dioscuri are battling to baffle a foul wrong, and we may presume, I think, that the god of gods would be fighting on the side of purity and justice and on the side of his children. I allude to the story of Helen and Theseus.

Let us turn now to poor Lakhsmaṇa.

His body was brought in, and at the suggestion of Jambavan, Hanuman produced a celebrated physician from Laṅkâ, who directed that someone should be despatched to a certain hill in the north, where alone, he said, a remedy could be obtained.

This mountain was called Gandha-Mâdana. It was declared to be part of the mountain Meru, which springs up from the centre of the world. Hanuman himself was deputed to go and fetch the desired simples.

But Râvaṇa got by some magical means to know of this mission, and he had an uncle, a great enchanter, named Kâla Nemi. A plot was hatched to destroy Hanuman. Kâla Nemi preceded him to the Gandha-Mâdana mountain. He disguised himself as a hermit devotee, and accosted the monkey magician, inviting him to his hermitage. Hanuman refused, and went to bathe in a neighbouring tank. A huge crocodile seized his foot, and a great struggle ensued. The crocodile was dragged out of the water and destroyed; but lo and behold! from its carcase emerged a beautiful woman. By a spell from Daksha, the son of the Universal Mother, she had been condemned to remain in the body of the huge reptile until released by Hanuman. She told him to beware of Kâla Nemi. Hanuman at once returned to Kâla Nemi and told him that he had discovered his treachery. He seized him and killed him.

Then the monkey, being perhaps a poor botanist, was at a loss when attempting to gather the revivifying herbals. What could he do ? Boldly he seized the whole Gandha-Mâdana mountain and carried it across India, herbals and all. This feat may shock University Dons, who in solemn black gowns allot prizes for masterpieces in Latin verse, but the groundlings are made quite mad with delight when they see the monkey and his mountain on the stage in India. The great dramatic festival of the Râm Lila used to take place once a year in the barrack square of my old Bengal regiment. Hanuman's feat was the most popular scene, with, perhaps, the exception of the waking up of Râvaṇa's sleeping brother, Kumbhàkarna, with tom-

toms, trumpets, crackers, the bellowing of bulls, etc. In real life the giant had a head as big as St. Paul's dome and a leg nearly as big as the geographical leg marked "Italy" in the map. The monkey army swarmed on his body in the fight like so many mosquitoes, and he coolly swallowed dozens and dozens of enemies, oxen, sheep, etc. He made only two meals a year, but these so exhausted the resources of the country that Brahmâ condemned him to live in hell. There he slept for six months at a time; then he woke up for a day, had a huge feast, and went off to sleep for another six months.

When called upon by his brother for aid against Râma, before he took to the field he drank 2,000 jars of liquor. He dashed down Sugrîva, the monkey chieftain, with a huge rock. In the end he was slaughtered by Râma.

Râma's Crucial Woe.

In the lament of Râma, one point perhaps may have struck the reader—the matter-of-fact, almost heartless, way in which he talks of Sîtâ. This certainly was my thought when I first read it. That is the crucial pathos of all. The proud Prince tries to hide the extreme depth of his overwhelming calamities—the personal question. Râma's love for Sîtâ is his life in epitome. But to that love has come a puzzle, a mystery, a crushing blow. In the zenana of the lustful fiend Râvaṇa has the daughter of Janaka been defiled? A second question, perhaps even more important than the first. Has she been seduced mentally by the diamonds and pearls that Râvaṇa captured from his brother Kuvera, the god of gold? These have been most appropriately stored in the lowest hell. Both these terrible questions have racked the poor Prince day and night. But now the great drama takes an unexpected development. Indrajit, the powerful magician of the demon hosts, carries on a battle in which success shifts from one army to the other. Malignant and powerful, he determines to wound Râma with a magical dart that no magical armour can arrest. By his weird arts he makes up a phantom of Sîtâ, and carries her along with him in his car to the centre of the invading hosts. "These saw," says the poem, "on the chariot of Indrajit, Sîtâ in bitter grief, with her long hair tied up into one knot, the *jâta* of the ascetics, defiant, worn to a shadow by fasting.

"At the sight of the woman of Mithilâ seated on that car, voiceless, her limbs sullied with impurities, it is said the bystanders were cut to the heart. Hanuman and the monkeys, believing that the demon was about to kill the real Sîtâ, shouted out furious remonstrances, which only amused the malignant Râkshasa.

"The son of Râvaṇa drew out his sword from its scabbard, and burst into a fit of laughter.

"When he had armed himself with this excellent brand, he seized the phantom of Sîtâ by her abundant hair. She screamed out the words 'Râma, Râma!' in heart-rending tones.

"Then Indrajit struck with his sharp sword the weeping phantom. As a thread, so was severed the life of this fair anchorite.

Her majestic form fell to the bottom of his car."

The terrible spectacle is too much for poor Râma. He falls down in a faint.

Death of Indrajit.

But the power of the magician Indrajit became more tremendous day by day. Monkeys and bears were struck down in thousands; and their officers, as in Homer, had to use very strong words to them to make them fight at all. Râma was despairing, and even calm and bold Lakshmaṇa, restored to life, was almost without hope. One day Vibhîshaṇa spoke very seriously to the Pride of the Race of Raghu:

"The success of my nephew Indrajit has a cause, O brave Prince, and that cause is magic. I have intelligence that to-night this potent and astute magician is about to work a terrific spell in the Chaitya of Nikumbhila. Should it go on unmolested, it is difficult to say what would happen. He would become invincible, almost omnipotent. I would suggest, O Pride of the Race of Raghu, that the hero Lakshmaṇa should be sent to attack him in the middle of his sortilege."

This advice was taken, and Indrajit was killed.

The Lament of Râvaṇa for his son has been compared to the Lament of Priam.

"O conqueror of Indra, valiant son!
First of my host! Say, whither art thou gone?
Thy whizzing shafts, controlled with deadly eye,
Tore the round shield or pierced the panoply,
And doomed each stricken chief in soaking blood
to die.
Earth was aghast. Confusion stalked around:
And all the war approached the Holy Mound;
The gods grew pale, the Ṛishis plied their spells,
Or fled disconsolate to hidden cells.
But gone these matchless feats—O bitter woe!
By fate arrested and young Lakshmaṇ's bow.
Proud Laṅkâ's rule was balanced on thy life,
Salt tears bedecked thy mother and thy wife.
What son, O Indrajit, shall tend thy sire,
Close his fagged eyes and light the funeral pyre?
From the wives' palace dismal sounds ascend,
As when two herds of elephants contend;
Complaint enormous, desolate and fell,
It wanders wave on wave through heaven and hell.
Lakshmaṇ and Râma boast upon the shore,
And gods on Mandar sleep in peace once more."

Râvaṇa now takes the field, undeterred by the remonstrances of Mandodarî his principal wife. The omens are unfavourable at starting :

> " With dust the world of sunlight is bereft,
> Foul crows and vampires circle to the left,
> And other shrieking birds, and from their throng
> A special group of vultures sails along.
> It followed Râvaṇ's car from spot to spot,
> As seeking prey assigned to them by lot ;
> His horses wept and from their nostrils came—
> Appalling omen !—lurid spires of flame ;
> Enormous serpents glitter in the brake,
> Wild dogs and wolves run howling in his wake ;
> And on the breeze from feasting jackal's throat
> Comes from afar a dolorific note.
> His pennon snaps, the monster as he rides
> Shows hues unearthly glinting from his sides ;
> Bright yellow, greenish, coppery, and red,
> The weird discoloration of the dead ;
> The God that holds the vajra throned on high
> With inauspicious meteors lights the sky,
> And at each pause of gloom and blinding storms
> Keen eyes can trace aloft appalling forms,
> As if the war had lured from blessed abodes
> Ṛishis and Siddhis, bright Gandharves and gods.
> And now great ruddy clouds are seen on high,
> All changed the swelling cisterns of the sky,
> Large drops come first and then a monstrous flood—
> Amazing omen !—'tis a shower of blood."

The Death of Daśagrîva.

More than one fearful encounter is described. He and Râma fight constantly together with enchanted weapons. Râvaṇa is killed at last.

"Now like a monstrous cloud when meads are bright,
That changes day at once to darkest night,
Once more the fated Daśagrîva came,
And from his mouth astounding tongues of flame.
Now right, now left, his chariot whirls around,
Shoots to the skies, or hurries to the ground.
Half animal, half human, are his steeds,
The legs of horses joined to human heads.
His shafts have serpent forms of fiery light,
But Râma's arrows check them in their flight;
One arrow lowers the demon's banneret,
A ghastly head upon a ground of jet.
From monkeys' throats loud shouts of joy arise,
Mixed with approval from the distant skies.
Another happy shaft struck off his head,
When lo! another figured in its stead.
Shaft follows shaft, and Daśarath's brave son
Strikes Daśagrîva's heads off one by one.
Then up spake Mâtali, the charioteer:
'Champion of Heaven, O mortal without fear,
Thy blows are vain. This ranger of the Night,
What boots it thus his many heads to smite?
Dost thou not see, O Pride of Raghu's race,
When one is lopped another takes the place?

Not thus his conquest on the battlefield;
His magic art protects him like a shield.
Take Brahmâ's Chakra, by Agastya given,
The Brahmaśiras, bolt conferred by Heaven,
Winged by the wind and tipped with Agni's fire;
It carries Mandar's weight and Brahmâ's ire.
Launch this, O Pride of Raghu, on thy foe—
Not thine, but Brahmâ's, arm will guide the blow.
Aim at his navel, through the armour joint,
His secret there—the vulnerable point.

* * * * *

Now see on Indra's car brave Râma stand,
The awful Chakra flaming in his hand.
Portentous issue, weird enough to scare
The gods upraised in crystal fields of air.
Râvaṇ is mighty. Râvaṇ's deeds of arms
Have filled the three great worlds with huge alarms.
Earth, heaven and hell—and now the crucial hour
Will show all flesh where sides the Almighty power.
Indra and Brahmâ watch the fateful dart,
And all the spheres are hushed to see it start.
Off speeds the Chakra to the demon fell,
Divides the steel and mocks each cunning spell,
Smites Daśagrîva with resistless force,
And burns and tears his navel in its course;
Then topples downward with a mighty roar
Th' unmeasured giant in a lake of gore,
And Laṅkâ's frighted isle doth shake from shore to shore."

On the death of the "Ten-headed," Râma announced that his brother Vibhîshaṇa was to succeed him. He also commanded imperial obsequies for the defeated monarch. Vibhîshaṇa conducted these, and the corpse, attired in its royal robes, was placed on a vast pile of scented chandan wood. Flowers and scented oils were there in profusion, and a black goat was slaughtered. Does not this clemency suggest another coincidence that goes beyond even the striking details of the births of Sîtâ and Helen? We have two Râmas, one who behaves in this generous manner, and the other who drags a living foe at his chariot-wheels, the last, however, only seen in the dream of an inspired prophetess. He was a symbolical prophecy, and not a man.

But the Homeric plagiarist has appropriated both these literally, not caring how badly they mix together. Achilles drags the living chief with his galloping horses, and offers up twelve human beings, in savage days when such sacrifices meant food for departed souls. And the same Achilles pays to his foe a tribute that goes beyond the chivalry of Marshal Soult in the presence of the dead body of Sir John Moore. Achilles, who, it may be mentioned, does not command the Greek army, orders a twelve days' truce between the contending armies, and sends back the dead Hector with much pomp, allowing the Trojans to fill the forests around, and pile up a "mighty sylvan structure," on which the body is duly burnt. All this was possible in Laṅkâ, but inconceivable in the scrub and marshland round Troy, when every little stick had long ago been burnt for fuel. And Colonel Muir points out, very appositely, that in the mind of a savage like Achilles, retribution to the dead as well as the living was one of the strongest of duties. M. Fauche holds that the obsequies of Patroclus were purloined from those for King Daśaratha.

Lakshmaṇa, in obedience to the commands of Râma, went through all the consecration ceremonies prescribed by the Śâstras, and unbruised rice, fried grains, sweetmeats and flowers were presented to the hero. Then Râma was reminded that no news had been sent to Sîtâ. Hanuman was despatched to

Vibhîshaṇa to ask his permission that she should be communicated with. The request was readily granted by the kind giant.

Soon in the Queen's palace arrived the monkey, and found Sîtâ sad and pale, and stripped of all the insignia of a high-born lady.

"Great Queen, success! Thy husband, the brave son of Raghu, has killed Râvaṇa. Did I not bring to thee a promise of victory when I flew across Varuṇa's wide domains without thinking of sleep or rest? No fear is there for thee to-day. Thou livest, O woman of Mithilâ, in thine own palace."

Sîtâ sprang up at the joyful news. She tried to speak, but happiness choked her words.

"What art thou thinking of, great Queen? Why dost thou not answer?"

"It is joy that keeps me silent," said the Queen in broken words. "When thou toldest me of the victory of my husband, O son of Vâyu, I was quite unable to sound a syllable."

"These words, O Queen, will be to thy

husband a joy greater than the joy of his victory. They outvalue a present of many jewels. These foul female demons that have guarded thee and insulted thee," said the ape, looking round at her guards, " will now suffer. I will tear to pieces their noses and ears."

" Do you not remember what the bear in the 'Purâṇa' said to the tiger?" replied the Queen, smiling. " The sinner alone can expiate his offence. These women were servants."

" What shall I say to the son of Raghu when I return ?" said the monkey.

" Tell him that his Queen has only one thought—that is, to see him at once.'

" With the joy that Śachî sees Indra her spouse wilt thou see thy husband, and he will see thee !"

Hanuman carried back the words of Sîtâ, but they did not produce quite the effect that the son of Vâyu expected.

Râma, on hearing the news, was silent for some time. A torrent of emotions seemed to struggle under his enforced calm. Suddenly he burst into tears.

"Let the Princess of Mithilâ be bathed and scented and dressed in splendid clothes. Let her be crowned with rich jewels," he said curtly; "then let her be brought before me."

Vibhîshaṇa impatient to see the union of the lovers, hurried off to the palace.

"Let me fly to him at once," said the Queen impatiently.

"No, no," said the good-humoured giant, who already scented calamity. "Better to obey thy husband, O Queen, and bedeck thyself as he desires."

Sîtâ allowed herself to be guided by Vibhîshaṇa.

And now a report got abroad that the beautiful woman of Mithilâ was coming out of the Royal Palace. At once all the soldiers of the conquering army collected to see her pass, as the Greeks clustered to see the beautiful Helen.

"What must this woman be like," they cried, "in whose cause myriads of the rescuing army have been killed? Has not a mighty sovereign perished on her account?

Has not a bridge, in length 100 yoganas, been plumped into the sea—rocks and causeway?"

As these words were being repeated, Sîtâ, in a rich litter, appeared, and all the bystanders were quite thunderstruck with her amazing beauty. Then, way being made through the thick crowds of monkeys, the palanquin of Sîtâ neared the presence of the King, but the poor woman was astonished that she received no greeting, though neither she nor anyone else guessed what tragedy was marching rapidly onwards to its fell catastrophe.

After a pause Râma, who had been giving orders about the crowding soldiers, said to Hanuman:

"These crowds come near to see a great lady. Why should they not? Let her get out of her palanquin that they may see her better."

There was a bitterness in these tones that all the Vanars perceived, and a mighty fear came over all, that as of an advancing calamity.

The Queen, pale and worn-looking, but

overjoyed, went modestly up to her beloved husband, and all were quite astonished at her amazing beauty. They said: "She is Prabhâ" (radiance personified).

Râma gazed at his wife for a moment, and then turned his eyes away suddenly, petulantly.

Sîtâ understood her husband better than anyone else. She had dreamt of this meeting on many a hard couch. She had prayed for it daily and nightly. Was it to become a torture greater than that of the Râkshasas of Râvaṇa in the Aśoka wood?

Suddenly Râma spoke:

"With my sword and my bow, noble lady, I have rescued thee from the enemy; it remains for thee bravely to perform thy part of the duties which matters require. I have quenched my rage and wiped away my dishonour. With the same blow I have struck down my foeman and his insults.

"A demon, in a borrowed appearance, seized and carried you away. This was Destiny. But these acts of mine are small. Every man desires revenge for an outrage.

"We crossed the seas. Sugrîva exhibited great skill and immense valour. Hanumân's efforts were almost incredible. The whole army was persistent and unconquerable.

"But take note of this, O woman of Mithilâ; all this has been done for my honour and not for thee. Thou hast been snatched from the hands of my enemy by me in my rage, but it was to wipe away the stains on the escutcheon of a noble family. They watch dishonour from afar, as we watch the star of Agastya (Canopus). It is something that the race of Raghu cannot reach. Your amazing beauty, O daughter of Janaka, once gave me great joy, but it now gives me great pain. We must separate never to meet again."

The poor lady of Mithilâ seemed quite beside herself with consternation and agony. She hid her face in the folds of her saree, and the movement of these folds betrayed her tears. Then, suddenly glancing at her husband, she said in broken accents, and in a low voice:

"Husband, dear husband, these words are

harsh. More than that, they are unjust. I have been true to thee."

But the moody imaginations of the King, suppressed and concealed in his inmost soul for many days, were now reaching the stage of madness; he said brutally, "Out, strumpet, carry thy cajoleries to Lakshmaṇa or to Sugrîva, or to Vibhîshaṇa, the chief of the Râkshasas."

The whole assembly were thunderstruck at this strange speech; and Vibhîshaṇa and Sugrîva came forward to remonstrate. The bulk of the Vanar army raised exclamations of dismay. But Sîtâ, who at first seemed dazed as if from a physical blow, now raised her hand and said in a low voice, beckoning to him: "Lakshmaṇa!"

"I listen, sister," said the Prince advancing.

"Thou hast said to me oft, that if ever I needed a protector, a friend, I could turn to thee. Alas! Thou seest that this want has now come to me!"

"Dear sister," said Lakshmaṇa, who felt for the Queen more than anybody there. "I love thee more than ever. We are not all ourselves this morning ; the fatal hand of the demon Râvaṇa is in everything ! "

"Brother," said Sîtâ in low tones which vibrated in the inmost soul of all the hearers, "my crushing downfall has come, not from the King whom I spurned and outbraved, but from the King to whom I gave a love that was at any rate all the love I had."

Râma had seen that his cruel speech had shocked all the auditors. He tried to modify it a little :

"Tell the Queen," he said to his brother, "that the Kshatriyas of the race of Raghu cannot put up with even the appearance of dishonour. The mothers of their offspring must be perfectly pure."

"And tell the King," said Sîtâ suddenly, "that it is right that the Kshatriyas of the race of Raghu should have the appearance of purity, but the race of the Devas need not seem pure. They are pure. My nurses used to tell me that I was Devi-born. At any rate I have ever lived my life as if that was the truth."

"Sweet Queen, all this is sad," said Lakshmaṇa. "It cuts me to the heart. Would you not get into your palanquin and come with me? It is better to keep quiet for a time."

"I will keep quiet for a time, O son of Sumitrâ. I will keep quiet for a long time. Dost think that I am ambitious to show myself for ever where folks can say: 'See yon false woman whose husband guarantees her dishonour'?"

"This cannot go on," said Râma to Lakshmaṇa, trying for appearance sake to speak calmly.

"It shall not go on, O son of Sumitrâ," said the Queen with dignity. "Construct at once a pile of the sort upon which dead Queens are committed to the god Agni."

These terrible words quite appalled the bystanders. Sugrîva and Vibhîshaṇa came forward to try and dissuade her from the mad act. Lakshmaṇa joined his prayers.

But a new woman now stood before them—a new Queen, erect, commanding, of surprising dignity. She advanced a step or two, and with a gesture enforced silence.

"The Śástras announce that a woman who is accused can vindicate her honour by an ordeal of fire. I demand the privilege."

"That is a fable of the Brahmins," said Vibhîshaṇa, who naturally was not a slave to their ideas. "It is a cruel fate for a poor woman. She is made to suffer the torture, and in addition has her reputation tainted after death, for no god ever brings the poor woman back to life."

"Back to life! Why should he?" said Sîtâ. "A few cruel words can kill a woman's reputation, a million cannot restore it."

It was a terrible tragedy, a fit dénouement to a combat of gods and demi-gods—blindness, cruelty, madness, a struggle too great for mortals. The outraged lady, in her pathetic frenzy, insisted on her privilege, and not a word could be extracted from the angry husband.

Vibhîshaṇa viewed the matter from the least superstitious point of view. His activity was immense. He made inquiries in the zenana of his late brother, and produced before Râma the woman Trijaṭâ, who affirmed that Râvaṇa had not molested Sîtâ, he believing all along that she would marry him directly Râma was killed. She mentioned also the incident of Sîtâ's refusal to escape with Hanuman, as it was held by the Brahmins that any contact with any male besides the husband was a defilement. Râma was at length aroused, and he rushed off frantically to the place of the burning. But he met his brother Lakshmaṇa, who described the last scene.

"Mark my bravery," said the poor woman, pointing to her jewels as she ascended the scaffold. "My husband ordered me to wear them. I die a Mahârâṇī."

CHAPTER VII

THE EVIDENCE OF DION CHRYSOSTOMOS

THE Greek writer, Dion Chrysostomos, believed that Homer had actually been translated into the language of India.

Says Monier Williams, Baden Professor at Oxford:

"The Greek writer, Dion Chrysostomos, who was born about the middle of the first century, and was especially honoured by the emperor Trajan, mentions (Or., LIII. 555) that records existed in his time of epic poems, recited by the Hindūs which had been copied or translated from Homer."[1]

Professor Lassen ("Ind. Alt.," III. 346) has urged that these must have been taken from the accounts of Megasthenes, who lived at the court of Ćandra-gupta, 312 B.C. This view of his is accepted by Orientalists.

Now, here we get the "Râmâyaṇa" and

[1] "Indian Wisdom," p. 316.

the two poems of Homer face to face at an early date. Ælian bears a similar testimony And the French Orientalist, M. Hippolyte Fauche, is quite convinced that the "Iliad" was borrowed from the Indian poem. And in the *Revue des Deux Mondes*, July 15, 1888, M. Émile Bumouf announced that the nineteenth century had experienced two great surprises: (1) The Indian origin of much that is called "Christianity"; and (2) that the Greek epics were not original, and that "even the great hordes of gods and men, and their muster to avenge the rape of a pretty woman, had been previously made into a great epic on the banks of the Ganges."

Professor Monier Williams tells us that "most obvious features of similarity or difference must strike every classical scholar who contrasts them (the "Râmâyaṇa" and "Mahā-bhārata") with the "Iliad" and the "Odyssey."[1]

Following up this idea, he gives several of these comparisons: The noble lament of Mandodarī for her husband, which reminds

[1] Monier Williams, "Indian Wisdom," p. 310.

him of the lament of Andromache ; Râvaṇa's lament for his son Indrajit, which reminds him of the grief of Priam ; then Helen pointing out the warriors of the Greek army to Priam reminds him of Vibhîshaṇa, pointing out the heroes of Lankâ to Râma from an elevated spot ; a dream consoles the forsaken Sîtâ ; and when victory has come to the followers of Râma, the monkeys crowd round her, admiring her incomparable beauty, the cause of so much danger, toil and suffering to themselves.

"The whole scene is very similar to that in 'Iliad,' III. 121," says the Professor, "where Helen shows herself on the rampart, and calls forth much the same kind of admiration."[1]

"The subject of both poems," pursues the Professor, "is a war undertaken to recover the wife of one of the warriors carried off by a hero on the other side"; and he adds that Râma corresponds to Menelaus, Sîtâ answers to Helen, Sparta to Ayodhyâ, Laṅkâ to Troy, Agamemnon to Sugrîva,

[1] Monier Williams, "Indian Wisdom," p. 360 n.

Patroclus to Lakshmaṇa, Nestor to Jâmbavat.

Now, most people reading thus far only, would think that the Professor had anticipated the present writer in his theme, and come to the conclusion that the "Iliad" had drawn upon the "Râmâyaṇa" for some of its inspiration. Not a bit of it. He holds that the two works are quite independent one of the other.[1]

Another authority, much greater, must be mentioned—Professor Weber. He, at any rate, admits connection:

"The rape of Helen and the Siege of Troy have served as a model for the corresponding incidents of the poem of Vâlmîki. . . . I content myself with the simple assumption that, in consequence of the mutual relations which Alexander's expedition into India brought about, some kind of knowledge of the substance of the Homeric story found its way to India."[2]

I have already contrasted the plot of the

[1] Monier Williams, "Indian Wisdom," p. 424 *et seq.*

[2] See also "Indian Epics," p. 16 n.

"Iliad" and the plot of Râma's story in Chapter I. In one, Râma, with Indra's chariot and horses and the charioteer Mâtali, advances straight to the ravisher of his wife, and slaughters him with a special weapon—the Brahmaśiras; in the other, the hero has Jove's chariot and horses and a charioteer who alone can guide them. Also there is a special arrow that alone can slaughter the ravisher of Helen. But everything goes awry. The arrow of Philoctetes is left behind, and Jove's favourite son is killed by the aid of the celestial horses instead of the ravisher.

Then the grave crisis in India is due to a disturbing fiend, who by mistake has been rendered invulnerable, and only a mortal can kill him. In the Greek story it is the Avenger that has been dipped in the Styx, and he prates all the time about dying too young, and sulks near the ships, and allows half of them to be burnt by the foe. Then the invulnerable avenger meets the vulnerable ravisher, but the invulnerable avenger succumbs, instead of Paris, the guilty offender.

Putting these two stories by each other—the one consecutive, pre-arranged, sympathetic, probing man's schemes and sorrows to their inmost depths; and the other contradictory, straggling, each incident the whim of the moment—we may ask which is the original and which the copy. Some ideas, as Herbert Spencer has told us, are "unthinkable." One such I take to be this: that a grave Asiatic should select this second splintered plot, and try to make up with it a Bible for 250,000,000 souls—the Book of Genesis of Hindustan.

Professor Jacobi.

Whenever I mentioncd the contention of this work to anyone taking an interest in Indian antiquities, the name of Professor Weber was thrown in my teeth. But another authority—a decisive authority—was also mentioned, Professor Jacobi.

There are one hundred and one points of contact between the "Râmâyaṇa" and Homer, but the Professor only admits one—

the bow used by Râma and also by Ulysses. He admits this one incident, but superciliously denies the remaining hundred. But what would be said of Counsel who begged the question in this manner in a law court? Not long ago the sum of £2,000 was at stake on the authorship of two plays. Let us suppose that a similar sum was staked on the question whether Homer had pirated the work of Vâlmîki. Let us suppose, too, that when the Counsel for Vâlmîki had set forth at length his claims, the Counsel for Homer adopted the contemptuous tone of Professor Jacobi, and "refused to take up the time of the Court in discussing mere coincidences!"

Would not the Judge open wide his eyes and cry: "Mere coincidences, gentlemen! What am I to judge by except coincidences?" Literary piracy and coincidences are identical words. One story has for heroine a beautiful lady born of a swan, with the Ruler of the Universe for male parent. The other story has for heroine a beautiful lady born of a swan, with the Ruler of the Universe for

HANUMAN (*p.* 115)

THE INDIAN MARS (*p.* 273)

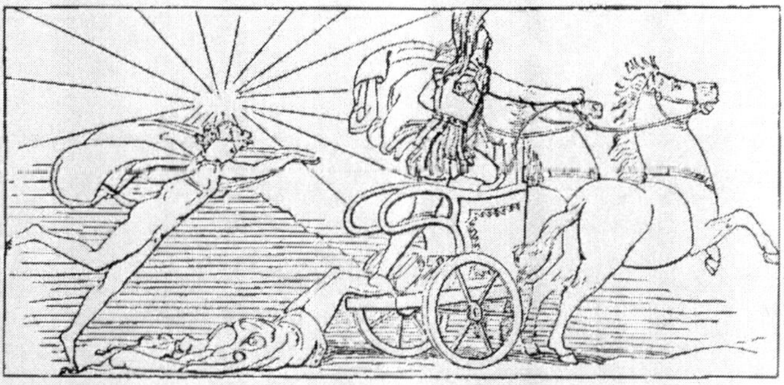

HECTOR'S BODY AT THE CAR OF ACHILLES. (*p.* 161)

[Face *p.* 180

parent. The spot whence one of these ladies emerged from her egg was called "Sîtâ" (furrow). The spot where the other lady emerged from her egg was called Ὑπερωον—an almost similar word. Both ladies after marriage were carried forcibly from their husbands; and large armies were collected to rescue them. The reputation of each was considerably damaged by all this; but in each case by-and-by a legend was invented that only a phantom of the lady had really been carried off.

"Now, it is all very well," the Judge might have added, with the fine irony that all Judges effect, "It's all very well for the defence to say 'Pooh-bah, that's the ordinary courtship of a Jack and a Jill!' These incidents have at least a superficial resemblance the one to the other!"

But Professor Jacobi relies much more on another fact: The word "Yavanas" (Greeks) occurs three times in the "Râmâyaṇa"; and the Professor gives many learned reasons to show that in each case the passage containing it is spurious. His object is a roundabout one, to show that no body of Greeks were known in India until the advent of Alexander the Great, and, therefore, Greece had no access to the great Indian epic.

But is not this placing rather a strain on the word "Yavana"; no Greeks might have come to India; but might not an Indian singer have wandered through Egypt, or along the Red Sea, to Greece? That is a point for consideration further on.

But Professor Jacobi starts one argument really important, but most dangerous to his theories. He holds that Helen in her own mind broke no marriage laws, for the Greece of her day had no knowledge of the sanctity of marriage. "The stealing of women in ancient times," he says, "and amongst a slightly civilized people, is a widely-extended custom." This is quite true. The Greeks were only a "slightly civilized people"! In the "Odyssey," especially, they show as wreckers, pirates, cattle and wife stealers. And the gods are as primitive in their ideas as the worshippers. As long as Chryseis is detained, Apollo slaughters hundreds of innocent people ; but when she is restored, he, like Chryses the father, seems to care little what has been done to her ; and with Menelaus we get much the same callousness. But if the Greeks of this date were mere pirates and wreckers ; if they viewed the stealing of women much as they viewed the stealing of sows and cows ; if Helen was what we call corrupt at starting, and the avenging kings and gods were accustomed to treat such matters merely as the robbing of goods and chattels, the whole plot of the "Iliad" is inconsistent and unmeaning to a degree. Why should many clans of wife-stealers cling together and battle for ten hopeless years about a paltry event that happened every day ?"

Professor Jacobi, writing in the *Nineteenth Century*, has for all evidence his own assertion that there is only one point of contact between the poems of Vâlmîki and those of Homer—namely, the bending of a bow in both poems. But the matter-of-fact Greek soldiers at the Seven Rivers (320 B.C.) dealing not alone with their internal consciousness, but with the nasal chants that come to them from every Indian bazaar, were quite convinced that Homer's poems and Vâlmîki's poems were translated the one from the other.

These Greek soldiers also wreck the main contention of Professor Weber that the "Râmâyaṇa" first appeared as a Buddhist parable, A.D. 400, and that the Homeric incidents were subsequently added.

I will give a sketch of the little Buddhist Jâtaka which the Professor deems the earliest version of the "Râmâyaṇa." Three children, Râma-Pundit, his sister Sîtâ-Devî, and his brother Lakshmaṇa-Pundit, are sent to a rude hermitage in the forest by their father Daśaratha of Benares, to escape a stepmother, who by "forged writings" plans their death. The changes in the story here, and their motive, are obvious. Sîtâ is made Râma's sister because a Buddhist celibate can have no wife. And the brothers are made "Pundits," though mere children, instead of bold warriors. "Sîtâ-Devî" also tells her story: she is a sister to a mere mortal, but she is a devî. The early Vâlmîki plainly knew all about Brahmî's egg. The King dies; and Bharata comes with an army to tell the news. Râma receives it with the extreme of callousness, exclaiming: "He who torments himself becomes lean and cheerless." (Can this author really be the Vâlmîki, who can still move two hundred and fifty millions of admirers, with his Dantesque picture of a mightly love in a Râma changing step by step to madness?) The story terminates, like all Jâtakas (or births of the Buddha), by revealing that Râma-Pundit is Buddha in an early existence; Daśaratha is King Śuddhodana, his father; Bharata is Ananda; and Sîtâ-Devî, the sweet wife, Buddha's companion through all the Jâtakas, the pure Yaśodarâ.

Now, I believe that if the learned Professor had lived amongst the Hindus he would have seen what a tremendous question he has here stirred up. It is quite enough to make the ample tract of land that goes by the name of Hindustan quake, as with a vast upheaval, from one end to the other; and its mountains to call out "Cover us."

For he actually maintains: That the Seventh Great Avatâra of Vishṇu, named Râma, was unknown in India until 900 years after the appearance of Buddha, who was Vishṇu's Ninth Avatâra.[1]

But all this is as nothing to what follows. The Professor gives to Vâlmîki a superhuman task—namely, to cull from Homeric records matter that can change his little goody-goody Jâtaka into the vast drama of the taking and burning of Laṅkâ, and the death of the ravisher. Supposing we give in to the Professor for a moment, and try to imagine Vâlmîki, with Homer's "Iliad" before him, setting about his gigantic task. To begin with, in the "Iliad" Troy is neither burnt nor taken, nor is the ravisher Paris

[1] The Professor also makes Kṛishṇa, the Eighth Avatâra, precede Râma, the Seventh. What would be thought of a Hindu in Madras, who, dealing with English history, announced that King Arthur and the Round Table appeared in the world two centuries after William IV., and William IV. seventy-three years before William Rufus?

killed by the injured husband. Then a Buddhist — for Professor Weber certainly presents us with a Buddhist Vâlmîki—would have to think of Buddhism. The great Śâkya Muni had given to the world a new ideal. He had proscribed bloody battles, bloody victories, bloody sacrifices. He had proclaimed that happiness depended upon the acts and thoughts of the individual, and not in a number of spells and priestly rigmaroles. Each Jâtaka (birth-story of the Buddha) describes him as I have said in a previous existence, and also his wife the gentle Yaśodarâ, who is ever by his side. What would be the wild consternation of the Buddhist community, Buddhism being still the chief Indian religion according to Hiouen Tuang, A.D. 400, if they learnt that this sweet ideal of womanhood had been shut up in the zenana of a foul fiend; a story that would go much further in mischief, for it would authenticate once more Brahman pretensions, Brahman hocus-pocus, and the Brahman regions of woe—in fact, everything that Buddha had come to earth to destroy.

Colebrooke, who had lived amongst the natives of India and studied their feelings and mythology, as well as their language, seems to have exactly reversed the teaching of Professor Weber. He pronounced that the life of Buddha was derived from the story of Râma. There are many points in favour of this contention : Buddha's education by Viśva-mitra ; his winning his bride with the bow of Sinhahanu ; his wonderful arrow that went through the seven Tala trees as Râma's did in the presence of Sugrîva ; the miraculous kick by which each young prince freed the country of a vast carcase which was poisoning the air ; Buddha getting rid of the dead elephant that Deva-datta had put in his path, and Râma kicking away a dead giant. Then there is the grief of the fathers that their beloved sons are to be anchorites ; the temptation of each young man by fiends, disguised as beautiful women ; the triumphant return of each to the "City of the King." The epoch of each was deemed also a Golden Age when the infirmities of humanity were unknown.

I will make one more jump, perhaps a wild one. Let anyone read my account of the slab at the Sanchi Tope, which represents the burning of the palace of the Nâga King,[1] and compare the account given in the "Mahâwanso" of that event.

What would he find? That Buddha attacked the Deva of Devas (Śiva) with fire from heaven, which set alight to his palace, and which frightened all his Nâgas or Devas out of hell, without slaying one of them. May not this be a Buddhist version of Râma's expedition? That also set alight to Śiva's palace, with the tail of Hanuman; and cleared the place of wicked demons.

[1] Lillie, "India in Primitive Christianity," p. 248; also 275.

CHAPTER VIII

THE EVIDENCE OF THE "ZEND AVESTA"

THIS chapter will be devoted to this question: Is the "Râmâyaṇa" historical? and does the Conquest of Indra by Bâli mean the great alterations in the religion of the Vedas produced by its contact with the religion of Bâli or Śiva?

But there is a minor point. Max Müller holds that certain "Cyclopean gates"[1] were erected when the Aryans crossed the Hindu Kush, and, until the advent of Alexander the Great, India became a sort of rat-trap.[2]

[1] Max Müller, "History of Ancient Sanskrit Literature," p. 15.

[2] "No intercourse was possible, after the Southern branch of the Aryan family had once crossed the Himâlaya" (Max Müller, "Chips from a German Workshop," vol. ii., p. 32).

Thousands of rats entered, but not one ever came out again. Professors Jacobi, Weber, and Monier Williams hold much the same view, and they decry all possible connection between the "Râmâyaṇa" and the Homeric poems in regard to this.

When the Âryas parted at the Hindu Kush each carried away a religion which certainly seemed on the surface a pure polytheism. The hymns and praises of the "Zend Avesta" are addressed to water and fire, etc., and these are some of the "praises":

> "The Fravashi of the soul of the Bull . . . praise we."
> "The soul of the well-created cow, praise we."
> "The Fire, the son of Ahura-Mazda, praise we."
> "The holy well-created Wind, praise we."
> "The Sun, with swift horses, praise we.
> "All waters praise we. All trees praise we."[1]

It was very much what Mr. Andrew Lang calls a "worship of odds and ends." Turning to the "Rig Veda," we find a similar worship of opportunism. We have hymns to Agni, to Indra, to the Dawn, to the Winds, and also to the "frogs," the "horse," and to the "dice," the god of all the gamblers.

[1] "Avesta," pp. 90, 150-1.

We see also in both religions a tendency to make a Walhalla of the pots and platters of the sacrifice. The "Car of the Aśvins" is the basket that brings the cakes; the Soma, the curds and whey. The "Samudra," the awe-inspiring "waters," where the unseen god dwells, is simply the pot of water of the sacrifice. "The Venerable Mothers" of Agni are the two sticks that ignite the fire. The ten mighty brothers, that march in procession, ushering in the Soma-god, are merely the ten fingers of the domestic chaplain.

The invention of an intoxicating drink is in India attributed to Śiva. He is Somanâtha, the lord of the Soma. Twelve chief Śivan temples, or Lingams, flourished in old India, and the chief one was Somnâth.[1] The intoxicating drink was extracted from a plant peculiar to the Himâlayas called the Soma (*Asclepia acida*). The Western Aryans when they imitated the rite had to put up with a sub-

[1] In modern times Lord Ellenborough accentuated the importance of this Temple by carrying back its gates to India. They had been taken to Canbal by the Moslem rulers as a supreme insult to the Hindus.

stitute very much feebler, the White Haŏma. The word "Soma" also means "the moon," and was worked into the first idea by a statement that the moon is the abode of the immortal drink; and the horned moon is Śiva, whose chief emblem is the bull. Another name for him, according to Professor Weber, is Kereçâni (Protector of the Soma-juice).[1] But the analogy goes a great deal further. Soma Nâtha (the Lord of the Soma) being Śiva, is the Creator and Lord of the Universe, and this raises up a vital question. The "Rig Veda," though a bible of polytheism, also addresses the plant as God Almighty personified.

"Thou art the Creator of the world. We invite Thee to gain the intoxication of victory."

"Soma, the firm support of the heavens, swims in the vast Samudra" (the unmanifested portion of the Kosmos described by the Gnostics as distinguished from that lit up by suns and stars).

"Come, O Soma, for the happiness of

[1] Quoted by Professor Spiegel, "Avesta," vol. ii., p. 56 n.

Indra and all the gods. O Hindu, strength is thy gift."

"The God of the all-seeing eye kills the demons. Kill Vritra, and give us riches."

"The shining Soma begat in the heavens the stars, in the air the sun, on earth the waters."

"Send from the heavens abundance of rain, O Soma; give us strength in our battles."

But the marvel does not end here. The orthodox Eranian polytheists suddenly began to sing hymns to Haŏma (Soma), the "illimitable ruler":

"At the time of the morning-dawn came Haŏma to Zarathustra.

"Zarathustra asked him: 'Who, O man, art thou?'

"Then answered Haŏma: 'I am, O Zarathustra, Haŏma, the pure, who is far from death.'

"Then spake Zarathustra: 'Praise be to the Haŏma!'"[1]

[1] "Yaçna," ix.

We learn, further, that Vivanhâo, the father of Yima, first introduced Haŏma to this world in the Golden Age, when death age, cold and heat were not.

"On account of his rule men and cattle were immortal, water and trees not dried up."

Here are other pregnant passages :

> "Thy wisdom, O Golden, praise I ;
> Thy powers, thy victory,
> Thy healthfulness, thy healing power."

"For this, as the first favour, pray I thee, O Haŏma, thou who art far from death : for the best place of the pure (Paradise), the shining, adorned with all brightness."

"Hail to thee, thou who through thine own strength art illimitable ruler, O Haŏma!"

"Haŏma has diminished the rule of Kereçani. . . ."

"This Kereçâni would slay all increase, annihilate all increase."

Now, here we get at once three claimants for the introduction of Soma-worship :

1. The followers of Śiva. The Soma intoxicant was one of the three secrets in their "Mysteries"; the Unity of God and the knowledge of agriculture were the two others.

2. The Indian Aryans maintained that they brought the knowledge of Soma with them into Hindustan.

3. The Eranians also maintained that they got the idea from the Proto-Aryans.

Śiva.

Dr. Pope, the leading authority for the languages and religions of the South of India, affirms that the worship of Śiva is by far the earliest religion known to India. On the other hand, Professor Max Müller contends that this worship is quite modern.[1] He goes so far as to assert that it is no older than that of the later followers of Vishṇu; this is modern enough. Professor Weber has

[1] Max Müller, "History of Ancient Sanskrit Literature," p. 55.

affirmed that these Vaishnavas stole their principal scripture from the Gospel according to St. John. He alludes to the "Bhagavat Gita," and Professor Max Müller himself has supported the silly Neo-Vishṇu additions which have corrupted the text of the "Râmâyaṇa."

Mr. Gwilt, in his "Cyclopædia of Architecture," declares that man had three stages of progress: First, the hunter, who had no protection except a cave, and no food but what he killed; secondly, the shepherd who moved about with a tent; and thirdly, the agriculturist, who had learned to build in the open.

Applying this, what do we find? That the religion of Śiva has the best credentials for being the oldest religion in the world. Over 1,000 cave-temples exist in India, with Śiva's sex emblem, the Lingam, in every small grotto or room, and cave-dwellings can be counted by thousands; on the other hand, Max Müller's oldest religion, that of Indra, in its earliest literature speaks of the "house" and the "master of the house" (*arih*), and also of "barley." This carries the bards of the "Rig Veda" at once into the third category—namely, that of folks who knew how to grow corn and build in the open. India, from its profusion of natural caves, seems to have been the country best suited by Nature for this cave-dwelling and this cave-worship. Its early symbols—Durgâ as the tree and Śiva as the serpent—point to days when India was spread with jungles and the Indian was obliged to face the deadly jungle fever in search of food, and also the cobra (*Naja tripudians*). To this day that deadly snake kills yearly about 24,000 people. Some of its poorer worshippers, such as the Aghori, still live in caves and feed on corpses, and their ancestors did the same for centuries and centuries.

Professor Horace Hayman Wilson announced that the literature of the followers of the god Śiva had been very little presented to the Hindus. The legends were very old, but they were not presented in Sanskrit. This remark struck me when I read a passage from a learned professor which fixed at a very modern date the works called the "Tantras," which deal with indecent mysteries, human sacrifices, and other rites called "Left-handed." But may not professors push their erudition too far when they rely on books alone? For many centuries—that is, until the letters of the Indian alphabet came into being—the scanty hymns and parables of the Saivites were preserved by memory alone. Also Saivism was a Pantheism—a secret society battling with their Aryan deadly foes. Colebrooke tells us that when he was in India these objectionable left-handed rites were still secretly performed. All this seems to point to blind conservatism rather than to disordered promptings, a grossness made sacred by many centuries.

Does not the cave-dweller explain the cave-worshipper? He imaged a god exactly like his own savage chief. He brought that chief animal and human flesh—no other food was known—and this, fresh killed, would be more wholesome than flesh of a creature who died of disease; rude music, dances, songs of praise, would not be absent; and beautiful women, as naked as the ladies in the Andaman Islands, would dance in a ring around him. Polyandry or some other crude custom would determine the relations of the sexes.

Now, here we have the mysteries of Śiva. The temple was the cave of the living chief. He appeared in the middle of it, and naked women danced round him, not because they were wicked, but because clothes were not yet invented. His statue was rude, a lump of rock, rough, unhewn—the Menhir, called the "Mahadeo" in India to this day. The form of this god, which much intrigued Bishop Heber, was based on a fancy that worlds were created like men by the union of a father and a mother. Music, dances, songs of praise, and by-and-by intoxicants, the earliest known, would be abundant.

The evidence for the great antiquity is quite overwhelming. In the "Rig Veda" itself Śiva figures as "Ahi," the serpent, "Bala," living in a cave; and Dr. Muir has unearthed two passages which mention the worship of his emblem a little too archaically:

'May the glorious Indra triumph over

the hostile beings. Let not those whose god is the Śisna approach our sacred ceremony."

"Desiring to bestow strength in the struggle that warrior Indra has besieged inaccessible places at the time when irresistibly staying those whose god is the Śisna, he by his force conquered the city with a hundred gates."[1]

The Śisna is the Lingam.

Another strong point is the serpent symbol. Śiva and Durgâ were Manasâ and Sesh—both, like all early gods of savages, hurtful demons. By-and-by they became good demons, and serpents were petted. Egypt and Babylon took up the serpent symbol at this stage of development.

Reading Colebrooke's Life the other day, I was still more impressed with the strange infatuation of Max Müller in trying to sweep Śiva out of India altogether. Colebrooke announces that the only gods in his day really worshipped were four—Mahádeo, Ganéś, Déví, and Vishṇu.[2] The first three

[1] Muir, "Sanskrit Texts," vol. iv., pp. 345, 346.

[2] H. T. Colebrooke, "Life," p. 141.

are presentations of Śiva; the last, the modern Vishṇu, is a make-up of Brahmanism and Buddhism, and with Saivism for foundation.

Two theories are in existence of the fate of the Proto-Aryan religion after the "Separation."

The first is that the two halves continued for thousands of years with very little change in dogma or even in minute ceremonial.

The second is that the Indian half took up a number of new ideas and ceremonies from the religion of Śiva.

In favour of the first, popular writers point to the lofty monotheism, which the "Vedas" and the "Zend Avesta" both teach; although, in both cases, it is veiled with a surface polytheism. They point to the close identity of rites, going to the extreme of superstitions in the case of the Bareshma and the Soma.

Now, certainly, the "Zend Avesta" at once sweeps away this first theory. If you asked any one of the 250,000,000 who inhabit India this question, Who is the "Deva of Devas?" there is not one who would not answer at once: "It is our phrase for Śiva!" And yet this is the title given to Ahriman, the Supreme Evil Potentate in the "Zend-Avesta." And the Western Aryans not only attack him; they may be said to make unrelenting hostility to him the basis of their bible, their rites, their punishments, and even of their confession of faith.

1. The bible of the Western Eranians is called the "Zend-Avesta," but its more accurate title is the "Vendidad." This means, literally, the "law against the Devas."

2. Malignant ferocity has been carried to extreme length in the punishment decreed for these "heretics." Anyone who feeds off a corpse is to be skinned alive; Śiva's religion, starting when corpses were one of the chief items of nourishment, retains the ceremony of eating some, in its Mystery of the Dead Year; that means every worshipper of Śiva is liable to this gross cruelty.

3. Says Miss Ragozin: "The Yasna has preserved to us an important document—the

profession of faith which was required from each Mazdayaçnian convert, the true Avestan Creed."

This creed begins thus: "I curse the devas. I confess myself a worshipper of Mazda, a follower of Zarathustra, a foe to the devas, a believer in Ahura, a praiser of the Amesha-Spentas. I profess good thoughts, good words, good deeds."[1]

And the excommunications of these devotees included the Vedic gods as well as Śiva. I give the words of this excommunication from the "Zend Avesta": "I combat Indra, I combat Çauru (Śiva), I combat the Daeva Nâonhaiti from the dwelling, the clan, the tribe, the region."[2]

They consign, they run the evil witting wicked Devas to the bottom of hell, the dark, the bad, the evil.

According to all Persian scholars Çauru is an epithet of Śiva, says Professor Spiegel; and he adds: "In the 'Bundéhesh,' it is stated: 'Ahriman created out of the

[1] Ragozin, "Story of the Nations" (Media), p. 111.

[2] "Vendidad" (trans.), p. 94.

materials of darkness Akuman and Ander, then Çauru and Nakait, then Târij and Zârij.' "

And now to this question: Were the rites and ideals of the Proto-Aryans carried on with little change by both sections, after the Separation, to Vedic times?

The religion of the savage is suggested at starting by some observed fact. The difficulty with the Western Eranians is that their chief rites are plainly not suggested by any local experience. They had an astounding enthusiasm for a plant only procurable in India, making it into a god, although they could only get a bad imitation of it. This plant, the Soma, was procured from the *Asclepia acida*, of the family of milk-weeds. They could not have heard of it until the Aryan had gone a considerable distance beyond the Hindu Kush into India proper. And even then, for a long time, its existence was a secret of the Śivan mysteries; and its culture and sale in after-times were in the hands of the non-Aryan tribes.[1] The

[1] Ragozin, "Vedic India," p. 171.

Eranian substitute, the Haŏma, had very little intoxication in it. This may explain the bitterness of their assaults on Krishanu, the Indian Soma Nâtha.

For the descent of this great god Soma in the rites, certain little bundles of the sweet Indian grass called "Kusha" were prepared—the "seat of the gods." Again the Eranians were forced to accept a clumsy substitute — a bundle of big twigs — the Bareshma.

Another borrowing was more remarkable still. It is recorded that Durgâ once got so angry with Śiva and his flirtations, that she practised black magic, and became so powerful that she began to burn up the half of India. The gods hastened to appease her; and she consented to become the tree Śamî, from which the wood for the fire-drill (Arânî) was always selected. This legend is due to a time when no other way of getting fire was available. The Arâni is the Mother of Śiva, for Śiva is fire. The Indian Aryans adopted the rite, wood of the Śamî-tree and all; the word "Agni" being substituted for Siva. But the Eranians only carried over the superstition. They put a bundle of fire-wood on an altar already alight.

About Vedic monotheism, a controversy between Professor Max Müller and Mr. Andrew Lang may be remembered by the reader. The Professor holds that the early races, and especially the Indian Aryans, had, at starting, a solemn sense of the infinite. Their religion was a spiritual religion based upon the conscience. This inspired the Vedic Ṛishis to pour forth a noble revelation of the great First Cause. After a time with all religions there comes a "parasitical growth," a hocus-pocus religion, with silly spells, and worship of bundles of grass, fire-drills, jars of holy water, cow-dung—opportunism used homœopathically to every current event. The Professor holds that the "Rig Veda," more than any other book, gives us the best evidence of this primitive religion.

"The 'Veda' fills a gap which no literary work in any other language could fill.[1] And

[1] Max Müller, "History of Ancient Sanskrit Literature," p. 63.

he calls it in a sense the oldest book in existence."[1]

Mr. Lang rather ridiculed this enthusiasm for the "Book with the Seven Seals," and for this new reading of savage thought. He speaks thus of the "Rig Veda" as not being so very ancient:

"These hymns are composed in the most elaborate metre, by sages of old repute, who, I presume, occupied a position, not unlike that of the singers and seers of Israel. They lived in an age of tolerably advanced cultivation. They had wide geographical knowledge. They had settled government. They dwelt in States. They had wealth of gold, of grain, and of domesticated animals. Among the metals, they were acquainted with that which, in most countries has been the latest worked—they used iron poles in their chariots."[2]

Two American Sanskrit scholars—namely, Professors Hopkins of Yale and Jackson of

[1] Max Müller, "History of Ancient Sanskrit Literature," p. 557.

[2] Andrew Long, "Custom and Myth," p. 217.

Columbia also deny this exaggerated antiquity. They date the "Rig Veda" from 800 to 600 B.C. And when we take Professor Max Müller's dates and try and work them into his theories our troubles begin. He tells us that the "first divergence" of the Aryas occurred at least 5,000 years before Christ; and that probably we should have to go to geological jumps of years to get at the real figure. He bases this on the very small divergence that has occurred between French and Italian in 1,000 years.

But if a religion has been twenty-five centuries in existence, can we reasonably talk of its "infancy," and treat it as if it were still free from the parasitical growth that ends that early period? Imagine the Ṛishis year after year wearily joining in a pleasing comedy and pouring out their eulogies to Vâyu and Indra, knowing all the time that such beings were purely imaginary. Imagine the stern Adhvaryu joining in the harlequinade; but burning on a red-hot bed all "heretics," that dared to assert that there was a god superior to the rain and the wind and the "Holy Bull." Imagine the ruck of worshippers, all pre-historic Schellings and Fénelons and Fichtes, obliged daily to bring to the altar their curds and whey and their ghee, and pretend that they thought that the basket carrying these comestibles was the car of the Aśvins, sailing proudly through the skies.

What is the Śivan legend of Creation? Śiva is discovered sitting alone in chaotic darkness. Then, by-and-by, he creates a female form, the great Śakti. Philosophers tell us that she is his will personified. Their wondrous nuptials people all the spheres with gods and men; but these die out at the end of an age (Kalpa, the "footstep" of the great Mahâkâla); and oddly enough the Vedic Brahmans admit this transitory nature of their gods. "Many thousands of Indras and of other gods have passed away in successive periods, overcome by time; for time is hard to overcome."[1]

The account of the creation of the world in the "Rig Veda" has been much admired

[1] Cited from the "Rig Veda" by Colebrooke, "Essays," vol. ii., p. 251.

and often translated. I will give one more version of it, made from a very literal French translation, that of M. Langlois':

" Nothing was then—invisible or seen—
No air, no upper region, welkin bright,
No cloud pavilion; nor th' unfathomed sea
That girds the continents in large embrace.
There was no death, nor mortal after-dream,
And naught to cleave the daylight from the night.
In chaos couched, breathed *That One*[1] breathless eke,
Gloom piled on gloom, and waters without wave.
Then from his tapas[2] shining worlds appeared,
Ushered by Kâma[3] with the germ of life,
That seed that has for produce world and men,
Bridging what is and is not,[4] Ṛishis say.
Whence came this mighty fabric—whence these hordes?
The gods themselves came afterwards to life—
That One knows all mayhap, who props the clouds,
Knows or knows not."

Now, about one point here there can be no contention. We get the god of the Seshvara Sankhya philosophy—a god incomprehensible and apparently callous, dwelling in Nirvritti, the Buthos of the Gnostics. He is the Absolute. He cannot create anything,

[1] *Tad*, "one," the unit of the Phythagorean philosophy.

[2] Potency of the Yogi.

[3] Sexual love—the Indian Cupid.

[4] Sat and Asat.

for everything is already perfection. He cannot supervise mortal affairs, for those affairs have already been arranged by absolute wisdom. So a subordinate agent has to be set up. All this is plainly in the mind of the Ṛishi who composed the hymn. A second question, an inferior one, is left apparently unsolved. Was this subordinate agent male or female? In other words, do we get the Śakti of Śiva or his son Gaṇeśa, the Logos idea of India and Alexandria? The word Kâma, which means "sexual love" seems to point to the first suggestion. That it was not "Proto-Aryan," as Max Müller suggests, is proved by a real Proto-Aryan account of the Creation brought down to us in the "Zend-Avesta." It is Ahura-Mazda, the beneficent Asura, who creates everything that is good, and Aṅgrô-mainyus adds everything that is evil—the words, "good" and "evil," being adjusted by contemporary opinion. Thus, Ahura-Mazda creates water and beneficent rain, and Aṅgrô-mainyus gives ice and snow. Then Ahura-Mazda gives healthy bodies to humanity and healthy food, whereas

Aṅgrô-mainyus settles the details of digestion in a most shocking and filthy manner; and so on. Then critics like Mgr. C. de Harlez, who has translated the "Zend Avesta" into French, tell us that that work is chiefly a *grimoire* of protective and also aggressive spells.

"I drive away sickness. I drive away death. I drive away pain and fever, I drive away the disease, rottenness and infection which Aṅgrô-mainyus has created by his witchcraft against the bodies of mortals."

Says Mgr. de Harlez: "The multitude of Daevas in the Avestan world, the belief in their unremitting action, in their continual attacks, in the necessity of incantations and conjurations to defeat them, the superstitions such as that about the parings of the nails being turned into weapons for the Daevas;" all this, the Monsignor thinks, betrays an outside and Turanian influence.

Turning to their brethren, the Indian Aryas, matters seem no better. Says Miss Ragozin: "We have here a weird, repulsive world of darkly scowling demons, inspiring abject fear such as never sprang from Aryan fancy. We find ourselves in the midst of a goblin worship, the exact counterpart of that with which we became familiar in Turanian Chaldea. Every evil thing in nature from a drought to a fever, or bad qualities of the human heart, is personified and made the object of terror-stricken propitiation, or of attempts at circumvention through witchcraft, or the instrument of harm to others through the same compelling force."

Both Mgr. de Harlez and Miss Ragozin hold that this goblin-worship came from the Turanians of Accad. But why go so far afield, when in India itself was a secret society practising exactly the same black magic. I allude to the Tantric or "left-handed" rites of the followers of Śiva.

To sum up, we have seen that from the earliest times India had a pantheism waging desperate and ruthless war with every polytheism on earth. Its chief secrets were three:

1. It proclaimed a god, one all-powerful, the hidden force behind all nature, the creator and sustainer of the phenomenal world.

2. The second mystery was the Soma plant. Its exaltation was received like the voice, not of the earth, which comes to the solitude of the fasting Yogi.

3. The third secret was agriculture. Durgâ still presides at the great harvest festival, and the Hindus of all sects flock to it.

Now, 5,000 years ago, according to Max Müller, a nation of polytheists reached the confines of India and separated into two clans, one alone passing the borders. Each of these, on the top of their polytheism, are found to have accepted the three main teachings of the religion of Śiva—the monism, the Soma intoxication, the secret of agriculture. How did this come about? The most obvious, and to my mind the most rational, answer is that each borrowed it from the followers of Śiva, the most secret and the most active missionaries of the past—fearless, ruthless, unremitting. "No," say the disciples of Max Müller and of the rat-trap theory. "'Cyclopeian gates' prevented any communication. These three points were all Proto-Aryan."

But on which side does the evidence lie? Professor Max Müller has nothing but surmise to go on, and the other theory is supported by the Brahmans in the "Râmâyaṇa," which admits that Bâlî, or Śiva, conquered Indra and the thirty-three gods of Vedism. Then the Western Aryans watched their Indian brethren with a love and a hatred combined, something similar to that of the man who idolizes but suspects his wife, and their bible, the "Avesta," emphasizes a vast victory to Śivan teachings. The rat-trap theory seems to tumble completely to pieces.

CHAPTER IX

THE EVIDENCE FROM GREECE

PROFESSOR MAX MÜLLER is never tired of discoursing on the real origin of the mythology of Greece and Rome.

"The 'Veda,'" he says, "fills a gap which no literary work in any other language could fill."[1]

On the other hand, he seems to have the worst opinion of all the mythology "indigenous to India." It is full of wild and fanciful conceptions.[2]

The Professor seems to have prepared two packets, and labelled the first "Vedic Treasure"; and for the second perhaps he

[1] Max Müller, "History of Ancient Sanskrit Literature," p. 63.

[2] Max Müller, "Chips from a German Workship," vol. ii., p. 75.

borrowed the language of the good folk who play "Patience," and labelled it "Indigenous Rubbish-heap."

But here comes the puzzle, for the valuable Packet No. 1 never reached Greece at all. By some mistake Packet No. 2 seems to have been sent off. What, according to the early Orientalists, was contained in this packet?

1. Messrs. Burnouf and Fauche would answer: Epic poetry so like Homer in a hundred and one ways that his work is plainly a simple copy.

2. The "Theogony" of Hesiod, for the battle between Bâlî and Indra and Bâlî and Brahmâ is plainly the great Greek battle of the "Hundred-Handers."

3. Ample confirmation of Sir William Jones and H. H. Wilson, who announced that almost all the rites and religious customs of Greece and Italy were borrowed from India, such as the Uttarâyaṇa (twelfth night festivities); Dii Lares (offering to the Pitri); Mattu Pongal (cattle-blessing, as at Rome); the Holi, with its rough and indecent merriment, pelting, April-fooling, etc.

4. Ample confirmation, also, of Sir William Jones's other theory, that the story of Osiris and the Dionysiac of Nonnus also borrow largely from the "Râmâyaṇa."

The hero of each of these epics travels *in India*, which rather upsets Max Müller's undiscovered America theory, that Greece and Egypt knew nothing about that country. Bacchus moves about with Pan as a counsellor, and this is plainly Hanuman. Whilst Jupiter as a bull is seducing Europa, a monstrous giant with a hundred heads, named Typhœus, is passing near the cavern where Jupiter has hidden the thunderbolt. He is attracted by the smoke, and gets hold of it. This brings about a monstrous war in heaven, and the gods in terror flee away disguised as animals—Jupiter as a ram, Mercury as an ibis, Juno as a cow, Bacchus as a goat.

This means that the Greek gods, from animated marble statues, were made into the animal gods of India. Jupiter at last, by a trick, gets Cadmus, dressed as a shepherd, to play on the flute, and whilst Typhœus is entranced with the sound he steals back the thunderbolt.

5. The fifth gift of India to Greece was a Śivan temple, transported bodily—the cave-temple of Eleusis. It contained the three great secrets of the followers of Śiva :

(1) The existence of one Supreme, All-powerful God. (This was the crucial revelation symbolized by a tiny Lingam hidden away in a basket, the famous Cista.)

(2) The mystery of agriculture personified by the Greek Durgâ.

(3) An intoxicant.

These mysteries were kept secret under a pain of death. Cicero, in denouncing these mysteries, tells us that human sacrifices were a part of their unhallowed rites. There were songs, there were dances, there was an intoxicant—the Indian Soma, or some improvement on it. Naked women circumambulated the altar—women who, unlike the clothesless women of early India, had clothes, if they liked to wear them. The gross revel called Baubo Demudata may have been something like the Śrî Ka Chakra of the

Devî Bashya. But Śrî (changed to Ceres) was at first the name of Durgâ, although afterwards Vishṇu's wife stole it. That lady, in a car drawn by dragons—the serpents or Nâgas of Śiva and his wife—came in with much pomp, and brought to Greece the knowledge of agriculture. She called herself Rhea. Her son Gaṇeśa, as Janus, carried the same boon to Rome.

One more point remains: the close similarity between the Yogis of Śiva and the disciples of Pythagoras. Colebrooke, Sir William Jones, and Professor Hayman Wilson were much struck with these; and Mountstuart Elphinstone, the leading historian of early India, has also ably supported it.

Pythagoras was born about 570 B.C. at Samos. But other very wild legends are afloat concerning his birth. He was declared by some to be the son of Hermes, by others the offspring of Apollo—a fact proved by his possessing a golden thigh. He performed many miracles, and travelled in Egypt, and, as some say, in India. The great scripture of the Yogis of Śiva is the "Yoga-śástra" by Patanjali; Colebrooke calls him a "mythological being."[1] The same is said of Kapila, who is alleged to be the author of a separate branch of the Sânkhya teaching. Like Pythagoras, his birth was carried up to the gods. He was called by some a son of Brahmâ; by others an incarnation of Vishnu. But a fact more important is mentioned by a Hindu scholar, Sabhapati Maudaliyar. He declares that Kapila's work is said to be only a commentary of a work still more remote in the distant vista of time.

Colebrooke tells us that the word "Sânkhya," used to denote the philosophy of Śiva, is derived from "Sânkhya"[2] (numeral). Sir William Jones wrote an essay maintaining that this basis of numbers was to be accepted literally. The same is certainly said of the philosophy of Pythagoras. God was the

[1] Colebrooke, "Essay" ii., p. 241.

[2] "The Pythagoreans did not separate Numbers from Things. They held Number to be the Principle and Material of things, no less than their essence and power" (Lewis, "History of Philosophy," p. 65).

One, the All in All, the great ἀρχή. This is exactly the god Śiva. In the hymn about the creation from the "Rig Veda," that I quoted in the last chapter, Tad is the Pythagorean One.

These philosophers had ten "Principia" for the number Two—light and darkness, good and evil, male and female, finite and infinite, right and left, etc., this last pair the origin probably of the "left-handed" and "right-handed" deities and rites. This dualism is conspicuous in "Śaivism," the only religion that has tried to grapple with the problem of the origin of evil. The One-God in one form is Śiva (the Prosperous), in another, Bhairava, the Lord of Hell. The figure Three is also much worked—the three prongs of the Trisula, the Trimurti, the three eyes of Śiva, etc.

Says Colebrooke, narrating other points of contact: "The Pythagoreans, and Ocellus in particular, distinguish as parts of the world, the heaven, earth, and the interval between them. . . .

"Here we have precisely the (*swar*, *bhú*,

and *antariksha*), heaven, earth, and (*transpicuous*) intermediate region of the Hindus.

"Pythagoras, and after him Ocellus, peoples the middle or aerial region with demons, as heaven with gods, and the earth with men. Then again they agree precisely with the Hindus, who place the gods above, man beneath, and spiritual creatures, flitting unseen, in the intermediate region. The "*Vedas*" throughout teem with prayers and incantations to avert and repel the molestations of aërial spirits, mischievous imps, who crowd about the sacrifice, and impede the religious rite.

"Nobody needs to be reminded, that Pythagoras and his successors held the doctrine of the metempsychosis, as the Hindus universally do the same tenet of transmigration of souls.

"They agree likewise generally in distinguishing the sensitive material organ (*manas*) from the rational and conscious living soul (*jívátmau*); θυμός and φρήν of Pythagoras; one perishing with the body, the other immortal.

"Like the Hindus, Pythagoras, with other Greek philosophers, assigned a subtle ethereal clothing to the soul apart from the corporeal part, and a grosser clothing to it when united with body—the *súkhsma* or (*linga*) śaríra, and *sthúla śaríra* of the Sánkhyas, and the rest.

"They concur even in the limit assigned to mutation and change; deeming all which is sublunary is mutable, and that which is above the moon subject to no change in itself. Accordingly, the manes, doomed to a succession of births rise, as the '*Vedas*' teach, no further than the moon: while those only pass that bourne who are never to return."[1]

But the case for the identity of the teaching of Patanjali and Pythagoras has much stronger evidence. The Yoga was an apparatus, specially designed to push out of existence, in all lands, the crude polytheism of the savage, with its fat priesthoods and hocus-pocus rites. For this, Śiva's secret

[1] Something of this filtered even into the "Rig Veda," whose bards ignored any survival of man.

societies penetrated everywhere; and proclaimed a God, One, the All in All. But the Śivan teaching as known in India had one or two points that were grossly irrational. If these are to be discovered literally transferred to the teaching of Pythagoras, we get inconceivably strong evidence of identity.

The metempsychosis in its earlier form was hailed as a priceless gift. The strange and new feeling produced by the Soma[1] was deemed a proof that death did not end all. There was a life beyond for man, an eternal life.

But the metempsychosis of the Sánkhya philosophy was a colossal punishment, an apparatus of human torture arranged to endure through tens of thousands of hopeless years. It was a punishment, too, arranged for man before he could have committed any

[1] Soma produces the Amṛit (Sect. vii., cap. ii., hymn 6). We read, too, "Soma has a thousand eyes" (Sect. vii., cap. ii., hymn 1). This is plainly connecting Soma with Śiva. We read, too, that Soma, "like the Bull, the Monarch of the Herd, shakes his horns and shows his might" (Sect. vi., cap. viii., hymn 3). The crescent moon, being the Taurine, is Śiva's special emblem.

offence. A mortal is born; and his career is adjusted for him through an infinitude of re-births by an unintelligent Causation, called "Karma." He may be a sweeper, a Prince in satin, a mosquito, an arch-demon, gigantic in shape and with the head of a buffalo; he may be the god Indra; he may be a beautiful woman; he may be an old sow. Karma, or the Causation of his previous deeds, is supposed to act as an infallible judge, and to silently fix the exact punishment or reward that is due to each action. The pessimism of the ecstatic Yogi proclaimed that everything in the world of matter was pain; and this torture could only be avoided by the individual becoming so purified and etherealized by ascetic practices, in birth after birth, as to become, after many thousand years, entitled to the Nirvâṇa of blissful extinction. This is certainly not the Amṛit of Soma Nâtha. Some strong reason must have intervened. The fear of death is said to be the one common, absorbing basis of religion in all lands. Perhaps some phase of the persistent persecution that the Turanians received from the Aryas angered them beyond endurance, and made them strike out a deadly blow.

"God, I'śwara, the supreme ruler," says Colebrooke, quoting Patanjali, "is a soul or spirit distinct from other souls; unaffected by the ills with which they are beset; unconcerned with good or bad deeds and their consequences, and with fancies or passing thoughts. In him is the utmost omniscience. He is the instructor of the earliest beings that have a beginning (the deities of mythology); himself infinite, unlimited by time." [1]

"Kapila," says our author, "on the other hand, denies a I'śwara, ruler of the world by volition: alleging that there is no proof of God's existence, unperceived by the senses, not inferred from reasoning, nor yet revealed. He acknowledges, indeed, a being issuing from nature, who is intelligence absolute; source of all individual intelligences, and origin of other existences successively evolved and developed. . . . The truth of such a I'śwara is demonstrated: the creator of worlds in such sense of creation: for 'the existence

[1] Colebrooke, "Essays," vol. i., p. 263.

of effects is dependent upon consciousness, not upon I'śwara, . . . beginning with the age and having an end with the consummation of all things.'"

Now, both these postulates go out of their way to treat the Vedic gods as finite in time, and their hymns and sacrifices as utterly useless. Colebrooke quotes another passage, which proclaims that "sacrifice . . . is attended with the slaughter of animals . . . is not innocent or pure; and the heavenly meed of pious acts is transitory. . . ."[1]

The announcement spread everywhere that Śiva destroys the entire universe at the end of the Kalpa. This seems to have been the blow. It killed all the Vedic gods, but the word Amṛit had to be written backward in Śaivism, too.

Colebrooke shows that the Pythagoreans had this metempsychosis of the Sánkhya, with annihilation viewed as eternal bliss.

" In like manner the Grecian philosophers, and Pythagoras and Plato in particular, taught that 'the end of philosophy is to free the mind

[1] "Káriká," I.

from encumbrances which hinder its progress towards perfection, and to raise it to the contemplation of immutable truth,' and 'to disengage it from all animal passions, that it may rise above sensible objects to the contemplation of the world of intelligence.'"

"The professed design," says Colebrooke, "of all the schools of the Sánkhya . . . is to teach the means by which eternal beatitude may be attained after death, if not before it."

He explains a little further on that this "eternal beatitude" means "an exemption from metempsychosis."

Now, the Yogis of India had a valid reason for changing their prolonged life of promised joy for a metempsychosis of annihilation and despair. Some such change was necessary when it was announced that Śiva destroyed at the end of each "age" every living thing, including Brahmâ and Indra. But Greece accepted the preposterous Indian metempsychosis without any such excuse. This gives us, I think, the strongest evidence of all against Professor Max Müller's paste-

[1] Colebrooke, "Essays," vol. i., p. 250.

board "Cyclopean gates." Most people will agree with the Indian historian, Mountstuart Elphinstone, who thus sums up the question:

"It is difficult to deny a common origin when we find a whole system so similar as that of the Hindu and the Pythagorean, and so unlike the natural suggestions of human reason."

CHAPTER X

ANIMAL WORSHIP

I SAID in an earlier chapter that a Professor who looked over my work had raised a very important point. He held that no Sanskrit scholars could possibly admit any connection between Sîtâ and Leda. The "Vahan" of a god was merely an emblematical animal. Brahmâ's Vahan was a swan or, as the Professor declared, a goose; and the emblem was simply used to denote the accompanying god, without any idea of literal animal reproduction. I attached little importance to the matter one way or another for a day or two, and then a sudden thought flashed upon me, which seemed to show that my critic had started a topic of the full importance of which neither of us had had the least idea.

Very early man, when he obtained a rough

idea of cause and effect, soon saw that its laws were being constantly upset by some mysterious unknown force. Before his eyes were creatures of immense power—a tiger who could kill a man with a pat of his paw, a serpent who could swallow a buffalo. Small wonder that in all countries animals got to be viewed as gods. This animal divinity had, let us say, three epochs of development:

1. The gods as animals.

2. The gods partly humanized, like the Centaur, which in Greece was a horse with a human head, in India a man with a horse's head.

3. Animal divinity lapsing into heraldry; but this seems chiefly noticeable in India when the god and his religion are dying or dead.

Colebrooke told us, as I have already mentioned, that only four gods were worshipped in India in his day:

1 and 2. Mahadeva and Durgâ. Their Vahan, Nandi, the Bull of Śiva, is as much a symbol of animal procreation as their lingam-yoni.

3. Ganeśa. The Indians hold that he has a wife, the daughter of Visva-rupa. He has an elephant's head.

4. Vishṇu. But Vaishnavism has dwindled in Bengal to a worship of Râma alone. He and Sîtâ are believed to be a perfect model of what sexual love ought to be when transferred to the skies.

Now the idea that flashed upon me was this—that the "Râmâyaṇa," instead of dealing with sexual love in the third or heraldic stage, deals far more crudely and nudely with the first stage of animal divinity than any other work that I know of.

What is the story of the "Râmâyaṇa"? Sîtâ, a lady born of a swan, is carried away by a fiend. A supernatural bird, Jaṭâyus, who is protecting her, fights with beak and claws, but he is overcome. The fiend is one of a group of serpents and elephants (both called Nâga in India), and this race is called Nâgas, in the "Mahâwanso."

When Râma kills him, he is described as lying like a great elephant on the ground. His son Indrajit has elephant's tusks. The wailings of his widows in their palace are like the moanings of elephants. Then his arrows are not real arrows ; they are serpents that run about and poison their foes. Kumbhakarṇa, Râvaṇa's brother, is plainly one of these huge serpents which, according to Buffon, swallow a buffalo, and take weeks and months to digest it. One in Java, according to an authority named Leguat, was 50 feet long. Did not Kumbhakarṇa's breakfast take six months to digest? A shark with a colossal mouth guards the sea entrance to Laṅkâ. This shark, named Surasa, is killed by a supernatural monkey who allows the shark to swallow him and then bursts his belly asunder. Sampâti, a vulture, who saw Sîtâ fly by in Râvaṇa's car, tells the monkeys whither she has gone. She is tortured by female Râkshasas, Aja mukhî (goat-head) Haya mukhî (horse-head), etc., but comforted by a jackdaw. The horses of Râvaṇa's car weep at his downfall. Indrajit has four tigers in his chariot; that of Dhûmrâksha is drawn by wild asses. Owls, crows, falcons, circle round this latter general as he rides along. An enormous vulture perches on his standard.

Turning to the bears and the monkeys, are they not invaluable? The "Râmâyaṇa" has been written and rewritten, sung, altered, and resung. A great genius, Tulsi Das, exhibited energy enough, and, indeed, courage, to rewrite it from beginning to end; but no one has succeeded in erasing or "civilizing" these bears and monkeys. They dominate in all illustrations of the poem, whether on the granite of ancient rock temples, or the mud and gilt idols of modern bazaars. What were these bears and monkeys? Did not Brahmâ call the gods together before Râma was born? Did he not urge them to procreate, with Apsaras and other supernatural consorts, an army of gods and demi-gods? There is nothing "heraldic" in all this. Did he not thus people the woods with supernatural beings of amazing strength, who could carry mountains on their shoulders, and fling about gigantic tree-trunks and mighty rocks?

The bears have the habits of real bears,

although they are gigantic and supernatural. They have only one method of attack—namely, to close with their foes and squeeze them to death. The monkeys have the habits of real monkeys, although for cocoa-nuts and bits of stick they fling tree-trunks at their foes, and rocks as big as a four-wheeled cab.

We are allowed to see the household of one of these special monkeys. The ape, Bâlî, usurps the throne of his brother Sugrîva. Râma restores him to it. Sugrîva becomes the husband of a female monkey, called Târâ, his brother's widow. Does he view her as a mere crest on a tea-spoon, as our Professor would suggest, a blazon on the carriage of a stockbroker who has just bought a peerage? Not at all. Târâ had already given birth to a monkey-giant named Angada, who does good work in his uncle's army. These bears and monkeys go back to the first archaic sketch of the poet. We reach what we may call "the bedrock."

It is quite impossible to gauge the importance of all this to our present inquiry. The

Professors may be said to be fighting in the car, Pushpaka, from which combatants can discharge their arrows, but which remains in the gloom; and the gloom has helped them much more than their arrows. But, supposing that this battle-car is not the car Pushpaka, but only a Neo-Vishṇu imitation. Let us propound a few questions:

1. The Indian religion in the old days was a polytheism. The religion of Neo-Vishṇu is a monotheism, imitated chiefly from Śaivism. Neo-Vishṇu in bodily form, as Krishṇa or Râma, or some other Avatâra, rules the universe from the Himalayan Mountains, which were believed to be the centre of the Kosmos.

The first question, then, is: Does the "Râmâyaṇa" treat of only one god? Or did thousands of brilliant gods and demi-gods surge up to the battle-cry of Râma, from East and West and North and South, as stated in the poem?

2. Was there any animal worship in India at the date of the poem? and, if so, did these animals propagate? Or were the divine

animals, as a later Sanskrit scholar assures us, mere heraldry?

3. Was Śiva, at this time, the great enemy, of the Brahmans, and were the battles at Laṅkâ fought against that enemy, in a mighty struggle of the gods? Or was Śiva at that time viewed as the "Third Person of the Trinity," a post that he afterwards held in Neo-Vishṇu theories.

4. The shrewd and learned Professor Hayman Wilson tells us that in Neo-Vishṇu days religion became a mere mechanism; Sanskrit holy books were studied "merely for the sake of repeating the words, the whole time being taken up in silly rites."[1] Was Râma a mere mechanical toy, wound up by his priest? Or was he a man of strong individuality, born for a great mission?

5. Does the author of the "Râmâyaṇa," in old India, stand almost alone as a master of pathos and of dramatic construction? Or is his story the most nonsensical, higgledy-piggledy muddle that has ever been presented to the world in any lan-

[1] Wilson, "Works," vol. ii., pp. 49, 56.

guage? Two hundred and fifty millions of his countrymen annually answer this question.

6. Professor Monier Williams divides Indian religion into two halves—the religion of the Bloody Altar, which prevailed until the advent of Buddhism; and the religion of Vegetarianism, the religion of the Bloodless Altar. He declares that all through the Brahmaṇa period (800 to 500 B.C.) thousands of animals were killed every day."[1]

Now, these questions seem all answered by the Professors in their writings, and their answers are noteworthy, for in them we get, as far as I can see, the only tangible evidence they can bring forward in support of their confident pronouncement that the "Râmâyaṇa" is much later than the "Iliad." If the Neo-Vishṇu higgledy-piggledy is ac-

[1] Monier Williams's "Hinduism," p. 4. See also Asoka's Rock Edict, No. 1: "Formerly, in the great refectory and temple of King Piyadusi, the friend of the Devas, many hundred thousand animals were daily sacrificed for the sake of food meat . . . but now the joyful chorus resounds that henceforward not a single animal shall be put to death."

cepted, no doubt it was. All the Professors, in a more or less nebulous way, support Neo-Vishṇu.

Sir M. Monier Williams.

This Professor, in his analysis of the poem in his "Indian Epics," treats the Neo-Vishṇu interpolations as quite authentic; and his contention that the Indian poem is stolen from the Christian Gospels would be quite unmeaning, unless he is alluding to the fact that an Incarnation of the Supreme God figures in both.

Professor Weber.

This scholar holds that the "Mahâbhârata" stole a great deal from the Fourth Gospel. He holds, too, that the "Râmâyaṇa" is more modern still, although in this Professor Monier Williams declares that he stands alone. If the "Râmâyaṇa" is more modern than a work filched from the Fourth Gospel, it certainly does not belong to Old India.

Professor Max Müller.

This scholar tumbles about the Incarnations of Vishṇu in a more hopeless way than Professor Weber. There is a silly account of Vishṇu as Paraśu-râma, and Vishṇu as Râma, meeting on earth, and, like two schoolboys, quarrelling as to which is the best archer, and then having a stand-up fight. All this occurs when a third Vishṇu is Supreme God on earth, for the rule of the ninth Avatâra (Buddha), which began 500 B.C., has to extend, according to the Neo-Vishṇu theories, over 333,333 years. Max Müller authenticates all this.

He tells us, too, that the "Râmâyaṇa" "describes a war against the uncivilized inhabitants of the South." This short phrase certainly crowds together as many fallacies as a sentence of the same length could possibly crowd.

By the words "uncivilized inhabitants of the South" the Professor plainly means men and women (mere mortals) dwelling in Southern India.

1. No such people opposed the advance of Râma in the poem.

2. The monkeys and bears which the Professor calls "uncivilized inhabitants" came all from the southern jungles, and constituted Râma's army.

3. He is plainly unaware that they were all superhuman beings. The bears, for instance, fight by hugging. But Indrajit and the other Yakshas is each as big as the Nelson Column. With such the biggest bear in the Zoological Gardens would be only able to hug a big toe.

4. The phrase "uncivilized inhabitants" is a very unhappy phrase to describe the subjects of Râvaṇa, who lived in palaces of crystal and silver and white marble, plentifully sprinkled with the diamonds and emeralds taken from Kuvera, the god of wealth; whilst the "civilizing" Râma and Sîtâ lived in a hut made of broken boughs and dead leaves.

The Professor also passes this criticism:

"The epic poems offer no assistance to the comparative mythologist." Truly this is an imperfect description of the "Râmâyaṇa."

From Indian jungles sprang the main religious theories of Indian religions, of all religions. Early man lived in a cave, and his sole food was the dead bodies of men and animals killed with his bow. He judged that the animal gods around him required the same sustenance to prolong life. Religion became at once a give-and-take idea. Man sacrificed animals to God, and expected God in return to protect him from mundane evils. Blood was the most precious item in the barter.

An old work, the "Kâlî Ka Purâṇa," sets this forth. In it Śiva explains how the divine favour is to be obtained, and he declares that it is through sacrifices that Princes "obtain bliss and victory over their enemies." "The blood of a wild bull gives Kâlî pleasure for a year," but a "bird whose throat is blue, and his head red, and legs black with white feathers," is quite her favourite; and the Rohita fish "gives her pleasure for 300 years."

But it is when we come to warm human blood that we find her real sentiments. "An oblation of human blood which has been purified with holy texts is the Amṛita." There is a curious passage in the "Zend Avesta":

"'If one buries in this earth dead dogs and dead men and does not dig them up again for half a year . . . what is the punishment for this?'

"Then answered Ahura Mazda: 'Let them strike him five hundred blows with the horse-goad, five hundred with the Çraŏshô-charana.'"

This is called the sin for which there is no forgiveness.[1] It is evidently levelled against the burial rites of the followers of Śiva. It is especially laid down that a dead body shall be left to the "devouring carnivorous dogs and birds." Did these ideas come to the Proto-Aryans? A passage in the "Mahâbhârata" might be urged for this conclusion. When the five sons of Pandu became slaves their arms were concealed in corpses hanging up in trees in cemeteries. This would be no concealment unless the corpse exposition was general. Far from the "Râmâyaṇa" offering no puzzles to the comparative mytholo-

[1] "For this there is no atonement" (Fargard).

gist, they crowd upon him. What about the vast gathering of birds that came to watch the battle between Râma and Râvaṇa. The birds were all animal gods. Was this the first rude sketch of the spectacle? In the words of Pope—

> "The gazing gods leaned forwards from the sky."

Of the six questions that we propounded, that sixth is the most important. It is crucial. Was the sacrifice in India at the date of the "Râmâyaṇa" an animal sacrifice? To answer this question we must turn to the "Râmâyaṇa" itself. Râma's birth was procured by a great horse sacrifice.

To begin with, was it an animal sacrifice?—the Brahmanism of Pre-Buddhistic days, not the bloodless altar of Post-Buddhistic days which Vaishnavism had adopted from Śâkya Muni. All the Kings and all the gods were summoned. The most minute points of the ceremony were carried out: the "Ascension of the Fire" as laid down in the "Kalpa Sâstra," the "Expiations" as they were called, the "Libations," the offerings to the horse of flowers and perfumes. Kausalyâ, the Queen, made her Pradakshinas (circlings) round the animal. She was then led by the Adhwaryu, or officiating priest, and she touched its nose. She then lay down beside it for a whole night. This is animal worship, rude, crude, nude. Compare it with the horse sacrifice in the "Rig Veda" which is a history rather than a hymn. Max Müller confesses its modern extravagance. That of the "Râmâyaṇa" is ancient and rude. There is one detail in the latter which the "Rig Veda" does not give—namely, that a vast number of other animals were slaughtered with the horse. This takes it completely away from the region of Neo-Vishṇu.

Râma's epoch is called the "Age of Gold." In those happy times the earth was supposed to give forth its fruits without cultivation. Râma and his brother at Chitra Kûta erect a hut of leaves and broken boughs. Lakhsmaṇa kills a black antelope with his bow. They feed upon it, the wife taking the remains after the males have eaten. Lakhsmaṇa kills several other antelopes, and dries them in smoke for preservation. The brothers at their first meal give to the "gods and manes summoned on the occasion" their portion of the meat. Similar offerings are made when the smoke-dried venison is consumed. Plainly the sacrifice in the original poem is always animal sacrifice, and the brothers perform it although they are Kshatriyas. This, in the days of the religion of Neo-Vishṇu, would be the sin for which there is no forgiveness. Also in one verse Sîtâ makes an offering to all the gods. Remark, these gods are the same as the gods of the army of Râma—animal gods—a polytheism; whereas the Neo-Vishṇu religion is a monotheism. Another point is remarkable. In the Buddhist forest-hermitages vegetables are cultivated. But in the hermitages seen by Râma nothing of the sort is mentioned.

From Behar to Adam's Bridge the brothers do not appear to have seen a house; and Professor McDonnell, Boden Professor at Oxford, tells us that the site where stood Patna, the capital of India at the date of

Megas-thenes, is described in the "Râmâyaṇa" as a houseless waste. Also we hear nothing of the hideous idea, the pessimistic metempsychosis of the Vaishṇavas, that forces every mortal to go through thousands of mortal lives, all pure misery; to be ended at last only by a Nirvâṇa of annihilation.

The holy man, Sharabangha, dies and Indra and his Devas appear to him at death to carry him off to eternal bliss. I was struck, too, with a passage describing the furies that vexed Sîtâ. They say with glee: "We will kill you, and carry your body to the Nikum-bhila (cemetery), and eat you and have a dance." Does not this seem to describe a very early form of the Śivan Mystery? Indeed, the fact that every one of Ravaṇa's followers is described as an ogre, seems not a satire, but a plain realistic account of Śiva's followers in very archaic days.

And we have also now and then a passage which throws side-light on what I call "animal divinity." Certain ascetics were disturbed by a foul giantess named Tâdakâ, who possessed the "vigour of a thousand elephants." They sought the aid of Râma. The two brothers set out to help them and, when they reached the forest which she inhabited, they suddenly saw a "second forest" surge up in the dim mist. It was a "magical wood, tangled and impenetrable, where the tick-tick of the cricket was answered by the lugubrious howlings of many fearful animals —the lion, the tiger, the wild boar, the rhinoceros and the elephant." This "second wood" must have haunted the dreams of many poor Yogis. To this day many perish from wild animals in the Island of Sagara where the Ganges reaches the sea.

Neo-Vishṇu.

Then mark the portentous absurdity of the Neo-Vishṇu additions. All the gods and men having banded together in their extremities, to give to the world a mortal hero to baffle a weird spell, exactly what they did not want tumbles down upon them. When the days of Queen Kausalyâ are completed, a god—the Supreme God—comes forth, smirking, who seems to forget that his Neo-Vishṇu ceremonial has been completely traversed by an early Brahmanic bloody offering. Would not such an appearance be received by the Brahmans and their King much as a figure of Guy Fawkes might be received if it entered a High Church at Brighton on November 5 during "Mass"? Then take the love-passages between Neo-Vishṇu and Sîtâ. Recollect that this god is the creator, and also the destroyer of the universe. Like Śiva, at the end of a Kalpa, he sits on a lotus in the eternal waters with Lakhsmî for his Śakti and creates new worlds. The duration of the universe each time is announced as 4,320,000 years. It is divided into four Yugas. This would make each Yuga about a billion years. Râma with Paraśu-râma and Vamana occupy the second of these with their Avatâras. This means that each of these is a Supreme God in bodily form, present and supervising mundane affairs, for some 333,333 years.

1. Can we believe that this Almighty God

pretended that he had fallen in love with poor little Sîtâ, and married her?[1]

2. Can we believe that he allowed her to be carried off from him by a fiend, and to be tortured by female furies?

3. Can we believe that this omiscient and omnipotent God, knowing her to be innocent, pretended that he thought her guilty and carried on this comedy as far as the burning faggots, watching her slowly dying in indescribable torture, when his divine prescience must have told him that the "ordeal" would prove utterly useless; for, even if it is true, as one version of the poem asserts, that another Neo-Vishṇu appeared at the pyre and cried, "Sîtâ is innocent!" we know that even in that version the Vishṇu in human form, after a brief reconciliation, threw her over once more, and sent her to die in a forest hermitage. Another strong point upsets the Neo-Vishṇu theories of our Professors. Brahmâ figures as the Supreme God all through the epic. It is by his edict

[1] For how many of the 333,333 years would his marriage vows be thought to extend?

that no god or demon can slay Râvaṇa. From him also comes the subtlety that this edict does not include a purely human combatant. If he had not been judged the Supreme God at the time, all the gods and all mankind would have laughed at both these pronouncements. Brahmâ parents Sîtâ and comes down to give her the Amṛita. Brahmâ urges the immortals with their consorts to parent gods and demigods for Râma's great army. Let us ask one more question. Suppose that Professor Weber's account is true, and that the poem started first of all as a little Buddhist parable A.D. 400—that is, 700 years after Brahmanism had been deposed in India. Let us suppose, further, that in time Neo-Vishṇu developments were added by Vâlmîki. Why was Brahmâ seated by mistake on Neo-Vishṇu's throne? How was he there at all?

CHAPTER XI

A PREGNANT DISCOVERY

WHILST this was in the hands of the publisher I came across a passage in the writings of Grant Allen which I consider a pregnant discovery. If his idea can be established as proved it helps me very much. In fact it raises completely the green baize curtain which conceals the mysteries of Śiva.

The idea came to Mr. Grant Allen when studying an account of the spring mysteries of the Parias of India. This was given by Sir. G. L. Gomme in his work "Ethnology in Folklore."[1] In the South of India the Parias hold a festival called the "Pótraj," after the Master of Worship (Pujari), who conducts it. In a field belonging to the community there is always a Lingam, or

[1] "Ethology in Folklore," p. 22.

shapeless stone. For the ceremony this is now smeared with vermilion. It is dedicated to the worship of the goddess of the aborigines—namely, Durgâ. A sacred buffalo, which has roamed about loose, like the Jewish scape-goat, is on second day thrown down and decapitated by the Pótraj. It is placed before the Lingam with one fore-leg in its mouth. By it is an immense heap of corn and grain, also holy vessels, with a drill plough in the centre. The carcase is then cut up, and each cultivator receives a little piece to bury in his field. Blood and offal is then collected in a large basket, over which pots of cooked food have been previously broken. Then the Pótraj cuts to pieces a live kid, and throws them in; and a low-caste man called a Mang carries the mixture about the village, sprinkling it here and there to feed the spirits.[1] He is followed by all the Parias.

[1] Colonel Dalton gives the ritual of the Bhagats: "O Mahadeo, we sacrifice this man to you according to ancient customs. Give us rain in due season, and a plentiful harvest."

On the third day all the inhabitants "of caste," who have vowed animals to the goddess for the welfare of their families or fields, bring their buffaloes or sheep to the Pujari for slaughter. The fourth day is appropriated to the offerings of the poor Parias. Some fifty or sixty buffaloes are decapitated, and several hundred sheep, and the heads are piled up in two huge heaps.

"Many women on these days walked naked to the temple in fulfilment of vows, but they were covered with leaves and boughs of trees, and surrounded by their female relations and friends."

On the fifth and last day the whole community marches in procession to the temple; and the Pótraj, after a little buffoonery, seizes, and stuns with a whip which he carries, a lamb. Then the Pótraj himself is tied up with his hands behind his back, and all folks dance round him with noisy shouts. He then imitates an animal and seizes the lamb in the neck with his teeth, and tears the life out of it. The blood is caught on a dish, and he plunges his head into that dish. This mess, with the remains of the lamb, is buried by the altar. Then the Pótraj's hands are untied, and he is chased from the place. Then the heap of grain in front of the Monolith is divided amongst the cultivators, to be buried by each one in his field with the bit of flesh. After this a distribution of the piled-up heads is made by the musician or "Raniga," but a big scramble takes place for a certain number of them. Then a procession with music follows the head of the buffalo, which is carried round all the domains of the community.

Now, here we get the early agriculture of India. As Mr. Grant Allen shows, the main idea of the sowing festival is that a beast or a man shall be slaughtered for the benefit of the community. He is then buried in the earth with bits of flesh and portions of edible grain to support him in ghost-land. By this expedient, plentifully used in the Pótraj theatricals, famine, the chief dread of savage races, may be staved off.

But whilst Mr. Grant Allen was pondering

over these transactions a noteworthy problem arose in his mind. How did the early agriculturist discover that the seeds of vegetables, sown in the earth, will come up again, and in quantities much increased. This problem might not have been much of a difficulty in days when folks believed in miracles and inspiration; but it seemed quite insoluble in a Darwinian universe of pure cause and effect. We of course know well that plants grow from seeds. "The seed," says Mr. Grant Allen, "is the essential reproductive part of the vegetable organism."[1] Also some parts of a vegetable are good to eat and some are not, and it is the edible parts that are reproductive. What could possibly have induced a Paria or a Mang, with limited brains, to bury the edible portion and expect it to come up again.

Then came the happy thought of Mr. Grant Allen. The ancient burial of the year-god solved the difficulty. The year-god was in the ground with flesh meat and edible vegetables to support him. Then lo!

[1] Grant Allen, "The Evolution of the Idea of God," p. 275.

and behold the beasts of the field and the edible fruits and grains of the village multiplied exceedingly. This it was believed was the work of the benign year-god. Plainly it was his buried flesh that made food so plentiful, certainly not the grain. This was the discovery that Mr. Grant Allen made: and even he failed to see all that it carried with it.

But another puzzle must first be considered. "Sympathetic magic," says Mr. Frazer, "simulates the proposed effect."[1] This in India is called the "Dharna." A beggar, let us say, is angry with a rich man who has refused him help. He sits at the rich man's gate and refuses to eat, and the pet wife of the rich man begins to show all the symptoms of death by starvation. The poor man has effected a sort of transfer of sickness.

When I was at Penrhos, in Anglesey, I was shown a couple of frogs that had been pierced and then buried with the name of the proposed victim written on a piece of paper. Sympathetic magic is an imitation of some incident that the magician wills to be real

[1] "The Golden Bough," vol. i., p. 10.

hereafter. This strange belief is found in all lands.

Now, the Indian religion, the Jewish religion, all the early religions, believed that there were thousands of supernatural beings always working diseases, disasters and famines to vex and starve us, and that the only way to eke out a bare existence was to attack them with counter-spells. We have seen from the "Râmâyaṇa" how the Aryas attributed all their calamities to the magic of Râvaṇa (or Śiva), and we see in the same tome the Apsarases, or nymphs, of Indra vexing the Yogis. The story of the Śivan mystery, the story of the Pótraj, discloses an extensive and elaborate attempt to meet the spells of hostile demons with a vast scheme of sympathetic magic. The Pótraj was erecting a powerful monarchy; the Pótraj was organizing a powerful army for battle.

Now, here comes the importance of Mr. Grant Allen's discovery. Śaivism was a pantheism with special intricacies. Its great mystery is made to fill in every little corner. It is elaborate and exhaustive, but all is founded on a pure mistake. In India, in Persia, in Greece, wild and irrational copies of it have been made by polytheisms in days when folks no longer believed that a smiling cornfield was due to a piece of a dead buffalo. But see how important this is. We get the elaborate and intricate scheme of Śiva based upon nothing at all. Cicero blushes and is shocked at the S'rî Ka Chakra and at Soma Nâtha. In the Greek mystery this was an orgy, but the earliest Indian had at basis deep religious feeling.

And now for the question of animal worship. What was the head or front of the Pótraj festival? Plainly an animal, the buffalo. Its head is buried by the holy pillar, called by every Indian a "Mahadeo," and Mahadeo is the Indian name for Śiva. In my work, "India in Primitive Christianity," I show the importance of Śiva's head ("Avalokitishvara," literally, "Śiva looking down"). It crowns almost every arch in a Śivan temple, and figures usually without a jaw; and it looks out of every window on the rock-detached temples of Elora and Mahâbâlipur, which, at a date now quite irrecoverable, were cut out of rocky hills with a chisel 4 inches long. In Greece this formidable spell became feminine, as the Gorgon and the Ægis, her serpents and the goat's-skin betraying the borrowing. When Buddhism allied itself to the religion of Śiva, Avalokitishvara escorted the head of the Church from Buddha Gâya to Lhasa; and the other day, incarnate in a shivering old gentleman, it crossed the Indian frontier and called itself the Dalai Lâma.

Mr. Frazer shows that in all parts of the world sexual embraces were deemed to be an important item in promoting the powers of vegetation. The Minnitarees of North America called their spring feast the "corn-medicine festival of the women." In the New Guinea festival "Mr. Sun" is married to the earth amid a vast number of similar espousals.[1] The ancient work, the "*Agriculture of the Nabatæans*," describes the process in ancient Babylon in a very literal manner. I give the Śrî Ka Chakra from the Devî Rashya in my work, "India in Primitive Christianity," and

[1] Fraser, "The Golden Bough," vol. ii., p. 203 *et seq.*

refer the reader to that. But in favour of the Indian festival of the Dying Year some points are important :[1]

1. At Easter Śiva as the Year dies, but in a second he jumps up again as Balishvara, a baby covered with white powder, the ashes of thousands of dead ages, and Balishvara is a potent giant an hour or two afterwards.

2. We must remember that in Śaivism everybody is a sort of incarnation of Śiva, and all produce in Śiva's scheme is by the union of male and female.

3. In the ritual of the S'rî Ka Chakra the males are called each "Bhairavas" and the females "Bhairavîs." Bhairava is a popular name of Śiva.

4. Now, this spectacle of an army of Śivas begotten in a second in ghost-land by another army of Śivas fits into Śaivism, but into no other religion.

5. And what about Soma? Does it assist us in this inquiry? I think it is of immense importance. We must remember that its thrilling excitations were only deemed purely

[1] "India in Primitive Christianity," p. 237, et seq.

divine for a certain length of time. The Bhairava at the Śivan mysteries believed himself full of the god and the Bhairavî had no shame; in its stead she had a firm belief that she was pious and that her life was useful. One sees from Matter that, even at the date of the love-feasts in Alexandria, women in the semi-Christian sects — the Nicolaites, the Carpocrates, the Prodicians —imitated the Indian "brides of the god," and one pious matron, with the significant name of Agape, trained a following of Agapetes. The Soma, as long as its novel energy was deemed divine, created a genuine divine enthusiasm. It gave a great fillip to the followers of Soma Nâtha, and it boiled over into the hymns of the "Rig Veda" and the "Zend Avesta." But when it reached Eleusis other intoxicants had been discovered, such as the grape and the spirit distilled from the Indian palm. This is a very strong fact against the theory of Oxford Professors that the Homeric poems and the Eleusinian mysteries are immensely older than Sánkhya philosophy.

Now, some writers on folklore have maintained that man was the first victim of agricultural burial, and that the slaughter of animals was a modified version of it; but Mr. Frazer shows very clearly that the savage failed to detect much difference between the man and the beast.

The distinction between the natural and supernatural seems almost to elude the dull intellect of some savages, and even the moderns believe that man can take an animal form at will and a beast that of a man. To this day Moondahs of Chota Nagpur are believed,[1] says Mr. Gomme, to change themselves into tigers and to devour their enemies. In Kamschatka, when folks killed a bear, they worshipped its decapitated head with prayers and sweetmeats, and told it lies as to who had killed it. "Deities of vegetation," says Mr. Frazer, "who are supposed to pass a certain portion of each year underground, naturally come to be regarded as gods of the lower world or of the dead. Both Dionysus and Osiris were so conceived." Mr. Frazer

[1] Gomme, "Ethnology in Folklore," p. 47.

points out that at Cyzicus Dionysus was worshipped as a bull, with bull's horns.

What is specially noticeable in the Pótraj story? This, that the Pótraj is not a beast playing the part of a man, but a man playing the part of a beast. He is tied firmly up; a victim, a kid, is placed before him; he gnaws it as a savage tiger would gnaw it. The blood in his chaps is of immense value, apparently.

And, in point of fact, the word "Pótraj" is loosely applied. It bears three distinct meanings:

1. Durgâ, the village goddess, is called Pótraj in Mr. Gomme's narrative.

2. The Pótraj is also a sort of beadle, who keeps order in the ceremonies.

3. The same functionary shams being tied up and slaughtered as a wild beast.

Is it rash to conclude that in early days the beadle and the wild beast were one flesh?

The proceedings terminated with a Bacchanalian scene which certainly supports Sir William Jones when he asserted that the story of Bacchus comes from India.

A procession with drums and music follows the buffalo's head round the limits of the commune, and "all order and propriety now ceased," says Mr. Gomme. Dancing women jumped on the shoulders of the most respectable and gravest citizens, and the low-caste Parias and Asádis attacked them. The Raniga, or chief musician, headed the hubbub and abused the goddess, the Government, and all governing powers. This is immensely important. The year in the Śivan mystery figures as an age (or "Kalpa") of Śiva in miniature, and this means a cycle of deterioration until, by false government and bad rulers a vast change becomes necessary. Hence the mad battling and the fierce animosity of the Raniga. It is a revelation in sympathetic magic of Śiva as the Destroyer, and explains for the first time the modern Hoki and the topsy-turvy buffooneries of the old Christian carnival.

CHAPTER XII

COLONEL TOD

ONE of the most intelligent of the old Orientalists, Colonel Tod, believed that Śiva as Bala and the Baal of the Phœnicians were the same god. When he was staying at Saurashtra he noticed the name on many temples. There was Balnath (the Lord Bal), Mahâbâlipur (the city of the great Bali or Bala), etc., and the plateau of Sahyadri Mountains was called Mahâbaleshwar (the great Ishwara, Bala). In Egypt he was Bal, or Sit, or Typhon; in Babylon he was Bel; and in Gaul and the West, Belenus.

"What," says Colonel Tod, "are Bal and the Brazen Calf, to which especial honours were paid on the 'fifteenth of the month,' but the Bâlshwar and the bull Nanda of India?"[1]

Colonel Tod explains that the Hindus divide the months into two Pukhs, or fortnights. At the beginning of the Second Pukh, called the Amava, the bull Nanda is worshipped on the fifteenth day of the month. Now, we learn from 1 Kings xii. that Jeroboam made a golden calf and sacrified to it on the fifteenth day of the month at Bethel.

More recent investigations are fully confirming Colonel Tod; indeed, the subject is brimming over in popular treatises. Says Miss Ragozin: "Thirty-five years ago no one would have thought of connecting India (pre-Aryan India) with archaic Babylonia. . . . In the ruins of Mugheir, ancient Ur of the Chaldees, built by Ur Êâ (or Ur-Bagash) . . . who ruled not less than 3,000 years B.C., was found a piece of Indian teak. This evidence is exceptionally conclusive, because, as it happens, this particular tree is to be located with more than ordinary accuracy: it grows in Southern India (Dekhan) where

[1] "Travels in Western India," p. 54.

it advances close to the Malabar coast, and nowhere else; there is none north of the Vindhya."[1]

The same work mentions also that the old Babylonian name for muslin was *sindhu* and *sindhu* is the early name of India. And here is another passage: "Professor Max Müller has long ago shown that the names of certain rare articles which King Solomon's trading ships brought him were not originally Hebrew. These articles are sandal-wood (indigenous on the Malabar coast and nowhere else), ivory, apes, and peacocks, and their native names, which could easily be traced through the Hebrew corruptions, have all along been set down as Sanskrit, being common words of that language."

But this is not the end of it. Dr. Caldwell, in his "Comparative Grammar of the Dravidian Languages," points out that these words of King Solomon are at root Dravidian words, and that Sanskrit only borrowed them.

Another Biblical analogy has received

[1] Ragozin, "Vedic India," p. 306.

attention: "But ye have borne the tabernacle of your Moloch, your Chiun, your images, the star of your god which ye made to yourselves" (Amos v. 26).

The word "Śiva" varies in different parts of India. He is "Shiva," "Shivin," "Chivin." The French always call him "Chivin." Scholars saw at once that the Chiun was Śiva. His "tabernacle" is the pavilion - carriage of Śiva; his "star," the six-rayed star of Śiva, made up of the two equilateral triangles, Siva's own, and the same upside-down for Durgâ. And Dr. Vincent, formerly headmaster at Westminster School, in giving a translation of the "Periplus," a valuable little commercial work written about the time of the Christian era, opines that Thebes, Memphis, Tyre became each in turn leading city of the world through Indian commerce.

Another question remains. If you were to meet these two personages in a street—a street outside the purlieus of Oxford—you might think that they bore some relationship the one to the other. Oxford Professors will not allow this. One is the bizarre idea of Kârttikeya, the God of War. He is Śiva's son, and with Śiva's loose pantheistic personifications, in one sense Śiva himself. The other is the bizarre idea of Râvaṇa. Vâlmîki twice explains the historical basis of his poem. Bali overthrew Indra and Râma overthrew Bali. Now, Colonel Tod has shown that Śivan temples in Madras are called after Bali. The hell Sutata is ruled by Bali. And it is declared in the poem, when Hanuman first reached the straits, that Laṅkâ is Pâtâla, or hell, and that the mountain Mainâka, a submarine hill, was brought there by Indra to "shut the gate of hell on those potent demons who without it would escape from their prisons." [1]

And the little episode of Bali and Sugrîva is the "Râmâyaṇa" in miniature. Bali upsets Sugrîva, and is then shot by Râma, the wife being Mandodarî, without any disguise.

Then Śiva has a son, Gaṇeśa, with an elephant's head, and Indrajit, Râvaṇa's

[1] "Sundara Kānda," VII., 8.

favourite son, has also an elephant's head. "He who brandishes a bow similar to that of Indra, and who betrays in his mouth two appalling tusks, like those of an elephant, that is Indrajit the son of the monarch of the Râkshasás."[1] When he dies, his wives complain like elephants, and Râvaṇa himself, when killed, lies like a dead elephant on the battlefield. But Indrajit has two aspects; he is also the leading fighter of the Râkshasas. This connects him with another son of Śiva, Kârttikeya, the Indian Mars.

Then Râvaṇa has the same Counsellor as Śiva, named Nandi.[2] He wanders about with his wife Mandodarî in Kailâs, Śiva's paradise. Night comes when he appears. He is called "the cruel demon of night." When he becomes angered he is described as like "Śiva in a rage"; and from his wide mouth issue flames and smoke.

A final question is this: Did I give the real termination of the epic in my little sketch? I think I did. Vâlmîki had pre-

1 "Ayodhyā Kānda," XXXV., 9.

2 *Ibid.*, XXXVII., 8.

pared us for it already; when Râma makes his lament over Lakhsmaṇa's supposed death he goes out of his way to run down Sîtâ. From that point all works to a lugubrious ending. Her refusal to let Hanuman carry her home is for that reason inserted. And confirmation of this comes from a seventh book, the "Uttura Kānda," a book known to be a comparatively modern addition. That book affirms that after a mighty form seen in the fire had announced Sîtâ's innocence, she came to life again, and she and Râma lived happily together for a time; but evil tongues once more poisoned Râma's mind, and he banished his wife to Vâlmîki's hermitage. There she produced twins—Kuśa and Lava. These by-and-by grew up, and went abroad reciting Vâlmîki's great poem. This brings Râma once more to his wife's side, to see her die.

Plainly a bad ending was as unpopular in those days as it is now, for another attempt at exculpation was made, with a theory that a phantom Sîtâ alone was a prisoner with Râvaṇa.

A similar story was in Greece. Two plays of Euripides—the "Electra" and the "Helena"—affirm that Helen never was in Troy; but that a cloud, or phantom, was substituted for her. It was asserted that she was on the territory of Proteus, King of Egypt, all through the Trojan War. The Homer of the "Odyssey" must have heard of the story, for he makes Helen reside for eight years in the Court of King Proteus.

The question can only be settled by a study of Vâlmîki himself. Plainly these new endings destroy all his pathos, all his subtle construction; and they quite militate against the teachings of the higher Indian mysticism.

A word upon that: Monsieur Schuré holds that the story of Sîtâ and the story of Proserpine are the same. Both were carried to hell by the Lord of hell, and both rescued, for their stories taught the same truth, the descent of a soul into matter—a pagan "fall" and a pagan "redemption," as Monsieur Schuré puts it.

But are the stories the same? Proserpine is a goddess. She is never in the earth-life at all. And she has no "redemption" or escapes. She remains the most wicked fiendess in the world for six months every year. She is at once Durgâ as Kâlî, and also Ceres (Sanskrit "S'ri"). And if this earth is deemed hell, Sîtâ coming back would have to go to Lañkâ once more.

GLOSSARY AND INDEX

THE END